Consent

A. M. D. G.

# The Cry Is Peace

# The Cry Is Peace

*by*

## LOUIS F. BUDENZ

*Peace, peace. And there was
no peace.* —Jeremias 6:14

## HENRY REGNERY COMPANY
### CHICAGO · 1952

Manufactured in the United States of America
by American Book–Stratford Press, Inc., New York

# Contents

Erratum: page 92, line 12 from bottom, the name "Claude B. Cross" should read "Henry W. Goddard." In the Index, page 239, the reference to Charles B. Cross should be omitted.

# Acknowledgments

In preparing the manuscript, the author has had the aid of Godfrey Schmidt in reading the pages from a legal point of view and Dr. J. B. Matthews in examining them for accuracy of facts. The work does not necessarily represent their views. This volume has been an extra-curricular undertaking on my part and is not associated in any way with my university work.

L. F. B.

# Disarmed America

Our powerful nation, arming many countries throughout the world, is itself largely disarmed before the Soviet fifth column, its followers and friends. If any American wants to know why this productive giant, the United States, has been battered about so severely in the Korean war, he should look to Washington, D.C.

Stalin's greatest victories, which have brought 700,-000,000 people under his heel since 1945, were gained not on the battlefield, but here in our own country. Poland was not lost in Poland, but in our nation's capital, through the influence of such traitors as Alger Hiss and such innocents as Edward Stettinius. China was defeated not by military weakness, but by the policy of the State Department upon the advice given our national leaders by those in the school of Owen Lattimore, who described the Chinese Communists as "agrarian reformers" or champions of "Asia for the Asiatics."

Since World War II the United States has consented to handing over nation after nation to the Soviet dictatorship. Through the infiltration of many areas of American life, Stalin has so "poisoned the wells" of public opinion in this country that he has gained his immediate goals on nothing more than our own uncertainty and delay.

Nowhere are these Stalinist aims better illustrated than in the address by Lavrenti P. Beria, head of the MVD or Soviet secret police, in Moscow at the thirty-fourth anniversary of the Bolshevik revolution in 1951. This address ( published in full in the Cominform's organ [1] for November 9, 1951) acclaim "the peace partisans" in every country, including the United States, as the great hope of the Soviet dictatorship. This throws a new and strong light on the value to the Kremlin of the various "peace crusades" inaugurated as Communist fronts in this country, which have enrolled many prominent Americans as members and sponsors. These "crusades," which have been used as sounding boards in defense of Soviet aggression, are a continuation of the infiltration during World War II creating the conditions and popular opinion which led the United States to back Soviet conquests elsewhere in the world.

We cannot avoid all responsibility for these conquests. The hundreds of thousands of people slaughtered in Poland are a direct result of our "allied" policy, though Poland, too, was an ally. We agreed to Poland's subjugation by Soviet Russia at Yalta. We confirmed Soviet rule by later acts, and we did not even have the courage to speak up for Poland on the floor of the United Nations. If Stalin is today dispatching his faithful Chinese Communists to pile up American casualties in Korea, this is likewise partly of our making. For there are still men in high governmental posts who worked for the downfall of Nationalist China, who did all they could to bring about the victory of the Chinese Communists. If Korea was defenseless when Soviet aggression struck, it was Ameri-

---

[1] The official weekly paper of the Cominform, *For a Lasting Peace, For a People's Democracy,* is published in Bucharest in all major languages, and distributed from there.

can policy that made her so. Never has the United States in any forthright, effective manner taken up the cause of those subject nations, now under Stalin's rule, to whom we promised so blithely the Four Freedoms.

Out of all this, the United States finds itself engaged in a two-front war of great magnitude. For World War III, as Jacob Malik recently announced, has begun, carried on according to Stalin's pattern and convenience. Stalin knows he cannot defeat the United States in frontal war. He has studied our productive capacity, and is perfectly aware that this country can produce, in a given emergency, as much as the rest of the world put together. His is a more effective weapon, the penetration of our government and the influencing of public opinion by his agents, who, through their activities and advice, turn America's strength into weakness by causing uncertainty, hesitation, and fear.

Nothing could help Stalin more in his plan for world conquest than the spread throughout the Western world of the fear of Soviet Russia's military might. It is we who have unparalleled military and economic strength, if we use it courageously, intelligently, and realistically. That is what the Kremlin does not want us to do.

Nothing could help America more than a spotlight thrown upon the Soviet fifth column here, especially on the way in which it fans out among the concealed Communists. They are today our greatest menace, the most serious threat to our democracy. Those Americans who are inclined to cringe in their homes at every mention of the atom bomb would much better be employed in actively combating Red infiltrators in their communities.

The McCarran Subcommittee on Internal Security of the Senate Judiciary Committee has amassed a record of treasonable activities that should both startle and inform

Americans. I shall have frequent occasion to refer to the material made available by this Subcommittee. Through its revelations, as well as my personal experience, I can show that it was the intention of the Communist conspiracy to involve the United States and Japan in war while Soviet Russia kept out. I shall explain why the Reds were successful in persuading the United States to hand over the chief fruits of the Far Eastern victory to the Kremlin. I shall show how, while American boys were fighting from island to island across the Pacific, plans were laid to defame General Douglas MacArthur and bring about his recall. We shall see, also, how the Communists worked to remove from the State Department all key persons opposed to a "tough peace" policy toward conquered Japan in 1945. It was their plan, fortunately thwarted, that by such a harsh policy the United States would alienate the Japanese and drive them to seek the proffered friendship of Soviet Russia.

These schemes, as well as Stalin's aims today, are supported by prominent men and women in leading American institutions. The information I shall produce, which is only a small part of the entire story, will, I trust, dissipate the current illusion that the Communist conspiracy is failing. It is succeeding, I regret to say, far too well. The delay-after-delay won by the handful of Communists chosen for court action has given time for the building up of the fourth and fifth rings of "reserves," which the Communists always nurture and train in military fashion. Working underground, as they have always done to a considerable extent, their activities continue uninterrupted.

Stalin has gained his easy victories here because of the immaturity of our political judgment. His agents have been able to deceive us both as to the nature of Communism and its mode of operation. Communism is an atheistic and materialist philosophy, which believes that a paradise can be attained on earth, a "classless society" in which all hates and conflicts will cease. But this is to be attained by the method and morals of bloody war. It is to be attained by means of a world-wide armed struggle, conceived in hate and carried through without humane or civilized scruples, to the point of overthrowing all "capitalist" governments and establishing a ruthless world dictatorship under the leadership of Moscow. This gives to the Soviet objectives a fanatical determination to achieve world conquest, similar to that which moved the Mohammedans when they threatened Europe. The Kremlin will not be diverted from that aim, since this doctrine is the very essence of its being.

If our American leaders had understood this doctrine, and clearly conceived it, instead of vaguely going along halfway with it, we might have put some check on the ambitions of the Kremlin, and we would not now be involved in a futile and interminable war. Their ignorance of what is going on in the world may well be disastrous. Soviet Communism is determined, by its very nature, to wipe out all other governments and establish world rule. Its immoral and flexible tactics, its wide use of native traitors in every land, and its rigid centralized direction give it a power that menaces freedom everywhere.

Americans as a whole do not yet have a genuine understanding of how the Communists agitate for the current line laid down for them by Moscow. Most of our authorized investigations have been made for card-carrying Communists, and they have produced alarming results. Stalin's most effective representatives, however, are free from any vestige of party membership or association.

They present themselves in the guise of honest State Welfareists, or as champions of social reform.

Personally, I have no wish in this crisis to support either the Democratic or Republican Party. This account is not to pillory any particular individual who engaged in the Communist cause—after all, I was myself a conscious member of the conspiracy until late 1945. My story is merely an indication to the American people of their own weakness that made possible the imprint of Communist ideas and aims on American thinking and action in recent years. I am aware of the alertness which has distinguished the record of a number of outstanding men in public office. I also believe that those who are responsible for appeasement policies must bear the responsibility. This book is above all an account of Communist penetration into American life, made possible by a blindness to the character of the foe with which our nation now contends. Stalin's *Foundations of Leninism* (available in English since 1934) states specifically the necessity, from the Soviet point of view, of smashing by violence the government of the United States. There has also been readily at hand Stalin's additional book on *Marxism and the National and Colonial Question,* which has furnished a blueprint as to how the conquest of Asia would lead to the Soviet conquest of the world. There have been Communist documents, distributed freely by Stalin's followers in the United States, which reiterated officially the determination to achieve world Soviet dictatorship. These frank declarations of the Kremlin's objectives, from which it has never swerved, have been shunted aside in many well-informed and leading American circles, and the advice has been taken of those who misrepresented the Soviet position. That has led to the disastrous situation we have reached today.

The cry now, issuing from Moscow throughout the world, is "peace." For the last two years the front page of the Cominform's organ, which gives the directives to the Reds everywhere, has been emblazoned with "the crusade for the pact of peace" and "the world front of peace partisans." In Soviet terminology the cry for "peace" is but a cover for expanding war. This has tended to bewilder the American mind. And the bewilderment has increased when the forces of appeasement in our midst have used "peace" and the "averting of general warfare" as their excuse for yielding to Soviet aggression. This has prevented us from taking that firm stand which would have halted a foe bent on world domination and only thus opened the road to real peace.

Unless the American government and its people can come to understand these things quickly, and act upon them, we stand in danger of collapsing before Stalin as France collapsed before Hitler. Prior to World War II, the Republic of France built up a huge wall of concrete and steel, the supposedly impregnable Maginot Line. But behind that line, France was destroyed from within. Otto Abetz and his Nazi agents were responsible for some of this, but the major cause for French collapse was the work of the Communists on behalf of Hitler. Maurice Thorez, leader of the French Reds, gave the signal by deserting his post as a soldier and escaping to Moscow. Through many avenues of French life, the Communists spread defeatism and became Hitler's strongest weapons in the easy victory he won. Let us work and hope that our country will avert that fate.

LOUIS FRANCIS BUDENZ

*Crestwood, New York*
*May 1, 1952*

# CHAPTER I

# The Years of Folly

October and November, 1942, were golden months for
Stalin in drugging the American mind. He gained, in
that brief time, an advantage over the United States that
was to grow steadily during World War II and that he
retains to the present day.

Hitler had pushed the Soviet armies across Russia in
one of the greatest military conquests of history, and
Stalin desperately needed the help of the United States
to save his dictatorship. America gave it, amid the sudden, almost hysterical, applause of the American people.
What was especially surprising was the clamor of our
American statesmen. Men and women in important government posts vied with each other, day after day, hailing Soviet Russia as a democracy and Stalin as a man of
the highest integrity.

On November 8, 1942, Vice President Henry Wallace
launched the American campaign for Stalin's Russia.
Speaking at Madison Square Garden as the climax of a
three-day celebration of the Bolshevik Revolution, he
indicated that in many respects the Soviet regime was
more democratic than our United States.

"Russia has probably gone further than any other nation in the world in practicing ethnic democracy," he

declared. Then he turned to "educational democracy," saying: "It is because Stalin pushed educational democracy with all the power that he could command that Russia today is able to resist Germany." As for "equality of the sexes," which Wallace termed the "fifth democracy," he held that we had failed whereas Soviet Russia had succeeded. In a concluding outburst of fervor, the Vice President proclaimed: "I am here this afternoon to say that it is my belief that the American and Russian people can and will throw their influence on the side of building a new democracy which will be the hope of the world." [1]

Ignored by Mr. Wallace were the horrors of the slave-labor camps, with their fourteen-to-sixteen hours of labor a day under the most barbarous conditions, the existence of which has been recorded by the most reliable authorities. Forgotten was the 1933 famine engineered by Stalin, which had killed millions of the peasants. Forgotten, too, was the Kremlin's treatment of artists, writers, musicians, teachers, scientists—the whole of the Soviet creative and intellectual world. Those who failed to be aware of and endorse the Politburo's current dictums were, with few exceptions, driven to suicide or punished with death at hard labor in concentration camps.

The very fact that Henry Wallace, as Vice President of the United States, spoke on such a platform was a symbol of how unguarded American leadership had become in 1942, a wartime and non-election year. For this particular affair had been staged by the Congress of American-Soviet Friendship, which was nothing other than the

[1] Mr. Wallace's remarks appear in the *Daily Worker* of November 8, 1942, under the caption: "Highlights of Vice President Wallace Garden speech." All other references to similar utterances by Wallace or others in this chapter are taken from the pages of the *Daily Worker,* confirmed by other newspaper accounts, notably in the *New York Times.*

old "Friends of Soviet Russia" in a new dress, an international Communist organization. This has since been declared a subversive organization by the Attorney General of the United States.

This is not in any way to single out Henry Wallace for castigation. It is merely to indicate the eminence of those who converted the American people to a false doctrine. Senator Claude Pepper of Florida, for instance, had risen so high in the ranks of Stalin's friends that the *Daily Worker* declared him to be "the best man in the Senate." The 1944 Republican candidate for President, the late Wendell Willkie, returned from a special mission to Moscow to acclaim "our gallant ally," the Russians, without mitigation. He stated that he had been permitted freely to go through the Russian factories and talk to the workingmen. What he saw there indicated their loyalty to the regime and the freedom they enjoyed. His enthusiasm was unmarred by any reference to the slave-labor camps, where millions of our "gallant allies" were dying at hard labor and starvation—for he was not allowed to see them. He did not mention Stalin's dread, all-seeing secret police, which is a continual whip over the workers, although this system had been thoroughly exposed in this country.

Preparations for this wave of Soviet propaganda had been made months before. In February, 1942, Joseph P. Davies, former Ambassador to the Soviet Union, had declared in an address in Chicago: "By the testimony of performance and in my opinion, the word of honor of the Soviet government is as safe as the Bible." Not content with this, Davies proclaimed that Communism—which clearly denies God and religious faith—"is protecting the Christian world of free men," and urged all Christians "by the faith you have found at your mother's knee, in the name of the faith you have found in temples of worship," to embrace the Soviet Union.

In May, Wallace gave his celebrated "Century of the Common Man" speech before the Free World Association in which he linked the Soviet seizure of power in 1918 with the American struggle for independence in 1776 as milestones in the "march of freedom." His conclusion rang out: "The people's revolution is on the march, and the devil and all his angels cannot prevail against it." Thousands of copies of this address in book form, identifying Communist Russia with American democracy under the simple designation "people's revolution," were distributed to editors, libraries, and magazines. The enthusiastic response of American intellectuals would easily fill this book. Our daily papers and monthly magazines glorified the virtues of the Communist regime in Soviet Russia and, particularly, the stalwart character and high integrity of Joseph Stalin.

Many of the more prominent figures in public life were counseled by concealed Reds or by those long sympathetic to Communist fronts or activities. Wendell Willkie's eulogistic statement, upon his return from Soviet Russia, was written by Joseph Barnes, then connected with the Office of War Information, who has since been identified by five witnesses before the McCarran Subcommittee as a Communist or Communist agent. Others who grouped themselves around men like Henry Wallace and Joseph Davies, and even had considerable access to the White House, were the now self-confessed Red, Lee Pressman; John Abt, who refused to tell Congress under oath whether or not he was a Communist; Nathan Witt of the National Labor Relations Board, who was guilty of the same defiance; and, of course, Alger Hiss, Owen Lattimore, and others of their school of thought.

While much of this deception of the American people may have been unwitting on the part of most of our leaders—aroused by the fact that Soviet Russia was fighting Nazi Germany—nevertheless, they expressed officially no word of genuine knowledge or understanding in this period regarding our relations with the Kremlin. The Stalin whom Ambassador Davies had found as honorable as our Christian faith was the same Stalin who had broken every major international pledge. The first breach of his solemn promise occurred when the United States recognized Soviet Russia in 1932. At that time Stalin agreed that no subversive activities would be carried on within the United States. This was flagrantly violated by the continuance of the Communist International apparatus within our borders, by the sending of espionage agents here, and by the constant control from Moscow of the Communist Party of the United States.

In 1935, insult was added to injury when the Kremlin called the representatives of sixty-five Communist parties, including a large delegation of American Reds, to Moscow for the Seventh World Congress of the Communist International. President Roosevelt protested this open show of bad faith, but the Soviet Government responded with the false statement that it had no control over the Comintern. After protracted discussion, our Government was compelled to eat crow on this issue, since nothing at all was ever done about it. How much we did swallow then can be seen from the proceedings of the Seventh Congress, at which all the assembled Communists pledged allegiance to Stalin as their "leader, teacher, and guide," and vowed that under his guidance they would establish world-wide Communism. It was at that Congress, in violation of the 1935 agreement with the United States, that Dimitri Manuilsky, then a power in the Communist International and head of all subversive activities throughout the world, acclaimed Soviet Russia as "the fatherland of the toilers of the world."

After those golden months for Stalin in 1942, with "Stalingrad" as the battle cry, the way was cleared for a completely uncritical attitude toward his dictatorship. The most patriotic and practical-minded Americans were stirred. For instance, even an experienced business executive like Donald M. Nelson, War Production Board chief, extravagantly proclaimed on November 8, 1943, at a mass meeting held under the auspices of the Congress of American-Soviet Friendship: "I have come back from my journey [to Moscow] with a high faith in the future of Russia, and in the benefits which that future will bring to the entire world, including ourselves. . . . In my talks with Marshal Stalin, Mr. Molotov, and Mr. Mikoyan, the People's Commissar for Foreign Trade, I found a forthrightness and realism that are the earmarks of the practicing executive everywhere."

At the same meeting, the late Harold L. Ickes, then Secretary of the Interior, asserted: "To each one, regardless of color or creed or origin, the Soviet Union offers social, economic, and educational opportunities. . . . The Soviets consider an attack on any group of citizens as one against the whole section."

This in spite of firsthand and authenticated information available in English at this time of the slave-labor camps in which millions of innocent Soviet citizens were imprisoned—a tragic fact, incidentally, that Vice President Wallace also failed to understand.

Looking ahead, Ickes prophesied: "What of the future? We want peace and security. The Soviet Union and all the others of the United Nations want peace and security. Peace inevitably will come."

The American GI, far from home in the rice paddies of Korea, could answer that prophesy today in less eloquent language. He could testify to the cost of the deception our respected leaders practiced—on themselves and the American people.

One year later, in 1944, speaking also under the auspices of the National Council for American-Soviet Friendship, the late Edward R. Stettinius, then Under Secretary of State, declared: "As we have fought and worked together, we have come to know each other better, and we have found that the cordiality of our relations has grown." To which roseate view of future Soviet-American relations, Stettinius added: "I am certain that we shall work out whatever problems confront us in full realization that the greatest goals of each of us must be the common goals of both of us." The then Under Secretary of State had specifically in mind the postwar world and "the establishment of secure and enduring peace." Unfortunately, he was not aware that Soviet Russia had no goal that eventually could be "common" with that of the United States. Again a knowledge of the Marxist-Leninist "classics" and their declarations for forceful overthrow of our government was lacking.

The crowning expression on behalf of Soviet Russia was written for the Communist magazine, the *New Masses*, in 1943, by Senator Elbert D. Thomas, a leader in the United States Senate. He wrote:

In the future when we make an estimate of Soviet leadership, we will see that it is based on the finest of democratic principles, the cultivation and the development of the people by providing proper education, proper health, proper hospitalization. I cannot speak personally of any leaders of the Soviet regime. I do not know them. But if "by their fruits ye shall know them," we must call them true leaders of men.

In 1944, Thomas wrote in one of his books: "All close students were in agreement that Stalin had abandoned all hopes of world revolution or world conquest." The Senator warned in defense of the Kremlin that "anti-Russian forces . . . will make every attempt to discredit Russia, to throw doubt on her motives and intention, and to make Americans especially believe that Russia is the most to be feared of all powers. . . . They will make us believe that the Russians have deep-laid plans to rule the world, to change all governments by force, to absorb all Europe." [2]

Senator Thomas had unfortunately not studied, or taken seriously, the promise of Lenin in *State and Revolution* and of Stalin in *Foundations of Leninism* that the Soviet dictatorship would of its very nature overthrow the United States Government by force and violence. Nor did he seem to be too familiar with Stalin's repeated prediction of the existence of "two worlds," the one led by the United States and the other by Soviet Russia, which would come into inevitable bloody collision. I know from personal experience how badly the Senator from Utah was taken in by the Communists, for I was one of the Reds assigned to taking him in, along with Joseph North of the *New Masses*.

While the majority of those mentioned here as unguarded friends of Soviet Russia were Democrats, a number of Republicans also were members of the cult. As late as February 6, 1946, the *New York Herald-Tribune* quoted Senator Henry Cabot Lodge, Jr., as saying: "We want peace with them [Soviet Russia] and I am convinced

[2] The book referred to is *The Four Fears*, 1944, and the article appears in the *New Masses*, June 22, 1943. Prominent criticism of Senator Thomas' pro-Soviet statements appear in *Counterattack* of January 12, 1951, and the column of George E. Sokolsky, published in the *New York Journal-American* on October 27, 1950, and October 30, 1950.

that they want peace with us." This matter cannot be regarded, then, as a partisan political issue, and to do so would be tragic.

That so many of our leaders were likewise taken in was a triumph for the Soviet fifth column in this country. The war spirit would explain enthusiasm for an ally. Still, the history of the Soviet Union, augmented by the published pronouncements of its leaders, the atrocities of the Great Purge, followed by the perfidious pact with Hitler, should have been known to so high a State officer as a member of the U. S. Senate. They should have impelled him to temper his praise of a military ally with some indication of the nature of that ally.

The Communists, their pace set by the infamous Washington cell, ingratiated themselves with our political and industrial leaders and placed themselves in key positions where they would influence the thinking of these men and thereby current American history. Julius Emspak, National Secretary of the United Electrical, Radio, and Machine Workers Union, was placed on the National Labor Advisory Board which conferred with President Roosevelt, and from that vantage point gave the Reds invaluable assistance and information. Emspak's pro-Communist tendencies were known at that time, and since then he has been identified before the House Committee on Un-American Activities and the House Labor Committee as a leading Communist, going under the name of "Comrade Juniper." Confronted with these charges in recent years, Emspak has refused on the grounds of self-incrimination to state under oath whether he was or is a Communist.

Joseph P. Selly, president of the American Communications Association, known to have Communist sympathies, was appointed during the war to a sensitive post connected with our military communications. In 1951, before the McCarran Subcommittee of the Senate, Selly refused to state whether he had ever used false passports, whether he had ever gone under the name of Selkowicz, and whether or not he was a member of the Communist Party. His plea was that by answering he would tend to incriminate himself.

Lieutenant Andrew Roth, arrested in 1945 for the theft of secret documents in the *Amerasia* case, was appointed during the war, over the protests of the military, as liaison officer of Naval Intelligence with the State Department. He had a previous pro-Communist record, and in 1945 he published a book, *Dilemma in Japan,* which championed the Soviet position that the United States should favor a hard peace in Japan, which could only have resulted in driving that country into the hands of Soviet Russia.

Scores of other names could be added of Communists and pro-Communists who swarmed into key posts which affected government policy and public opinion. With such advisers and trusted government employees, it is not too surprising that some of our highest officers should have gone all-out for a dictatorship only accidentally engaged in war against one of our enemies.

While the glorification of Soviet Russia thus dominated the speeches of our leaders and the columns of our magazines and newspapers, Stalin was pursuing quite another course. Although formally our co-belligerent, he still regarded America as his foe. Throughout the war, in his orders of the day, he refrained from exuberance over the effort of the United States or Great Britain. For expediency's sake, he proclaimed the conflict to be a "war of national liberation," but he stressed that the Russian people were fighting "under the banner of Lenin." And that banner, as every Communist knows, is for eventual world conquest. By raising it, in his orders of the day, Stalin continued to remind his devoted followers throughout the world that Communism would triumph over all, temporary friend and foe alike.

While Stalin's cool references to his Western allies were noticed and criticized by our press, many newspapers began to explain it away by applauding the Soviet dictator's "progressive" views. The St. Louis *Post Dispatch*, for example, went all-out on Stalin's writings about the self-determination of nations and the right of nationalities in the Soviet Union to secede. These statements had been exploded long ago by the repressive acts of the Soviet dictatorship in the Ukraine and in other places. They had been caricatured by the Soviet invasion of Poland, in connivance with Hitler, and the "liberation" of the Baltic states by their forceful incorporation into Soviet Russia. The *Post Dispatch* nevertheless cited with approval the following pledge by Stalin with regard to Soviet war aims in 1941, which received wide and favorable publicity in this country:

We have no war aims of imposing our regime, Slav or otherwise, on the enslaved peoples of the world who are waiting for our help, nor can we have such aims. Our aim is to help these people, to liberate them from the Hitlerite tyranny, and then to leave them free to live on their own lands as they wish. There can be no interference in the affairs of other people.

The wrecks of nations behind the Iron Curtain today reveal how tragically naïve were the St. Louis *Post Dispatch* and other newspapers which credulously played up such statements without regard to the facts. The "right of secession" for divisions of Soviet Russia, to which these newspapers referred with such approval, has been revealed as completely fictitious by the Soviet Government itself. After the war it came forward with the belated announcement that four of its "republics" and one autonomous province had been snuffed out for disloyalty, their inhabitants scattered throughout Siberia. To get some idea of what this meant, imagine for a moment that President Truman in 1948 had decreed that the "Dixiecrat" states should be dropped as members of the Union and their populations deported en masse to Alaska.

This postwar announcement gave the lie to yet another of Stalin's previous declarations during the war—his boasting of the strength of the Soviet "rear." They also made comical the assertions by leading Americans of the "might" of our Soviet ally. Secretary of the Interior Ickes even exclaimed: "We may ask ourselves: 'Where would we be today if it had not been for the mighty Russia?'" That sort of language, repeated in public address after public address, came to be generally accepted. It remains today in the thinking, not only of those who can be called pro-Communists or appeasers, but even of some known anti-Communists. Thus, former President Herbert Hoover, in his now famous speech of 1950 on the United States as a "Gibraltar" of freedom, went so far as to say that Hitler had not been able to defeat Soviet Russia on land. The question that Ickes should have asked was this: Where would the Soviet dictatorship have been without the help of the industrial might of the United States? Anyone in the Communist camp during the war knew that Hitler had smashed the Soviet armies and defenses, and that Stalin was saved only by American lend-lease and Hitler's fear of American invasion of western Europe. Father Leopold Braun, who lived in Moscow during the days when the march of Hitler's armies reverberated throughout that city, has confirmed the fact that Stalin's forces would have been completely at Hitler's mercy except for American intervention.

Such pro-Soviet expressions as Secretary Ickes' were echoed or simulated by his colleagues in public office and by men and women who occupied other positions of prominence in the people's estimate. "Thank God for Communism," exclaimed Charlie Chaplin, when he arrived in New York on October 17, 1942. The screen comedian had come from Hollywood to be the chief speaker at a rally for the Second Front, sponsored by the Communist Party, at which he praised Stalin and Soviet Russia without stint. Two days later, in an interview with the *Daily Worker,* Chaplin added: "They say Communism may spread out all over the world. And I say: 'So what?' Yes, who knows what is going to happen after the war?"

Chaplin's unrestrained utterances were not too surprising. Although he had risen to wealth and prominence in this country, he had rejected American citizenship, proclaiming himself a "citizen of the world." During the production of his last silent film, *Modern Times,* he had submitted his text, according to the *Daily Worker,* to the Moscow Cinema Board.

Within a few months, he was joined on the pro-Soviet bandwagon by Marshall Field, the Chicago millionaire, who had initiated several liberal newspapers. In an address at the Russian War Relief luncheon on December 16, 1942, Field declared that the time had come to "blow away the mists of suspicion" which Americans had about Soviet Russia. "We must learn our lesson well," Field stated. "If we have lost sixty per cent of our old fear of Russia, we have got to lose the other forty per cent, too. . . . We must remember that the Russian form of government apparently pleases the Russian people very much indeed." To which the Chicago millionaire added his firm belief that Soviet Russia would be "a constructive influence for peace in the new world."

As a symbol of the way things went among those who made public opinion, the poet Archibald MacLeish signalized his appointment as Assistant Secretary of State by making his first public appearance thereafter before a Communist front on February 18, 1945. It was at a Political Action Committee dinner of the Independent Citizens Committee of the Arts, Sciences, and Professions, an organization formed by the Communists and their friends in the wake of the war enthusiasm for Soviet Russia and the Communist cause. On this occasion, Mr. MacLeish sharply took issue with those who criticized "our allies" in the war.

It is true, of course, that the attack by Japan upon Pearl Harbor provides some excuse for this pro-Soviet enthusiasm of so many men in American public life. They did not know then that Soviet Russia was covertly inciting both the United States and Japan to attack each other. The McCarran hearings have raised the curtain on the Soviet espionage ring headed by the German, Richard Sorge, which reached into high places in Japan and provoked leading Japanese figures to attack the United States. The McCarran investigation has also shown that here in the United States the Communists and pro-Communists were taking advantage of their infiltration of the Institute of Pacific Relations to bring pressure in Washington to needle Japan. However, those who uncritically praised Soviet Russia might have recalled that Stalin in 1939 had predicted that "the encirclement of socialism by capitalism" would be followed by the "encirclement of capitalism by socialism." That could only mean a two-front war against the United States, the leading "capitalist" nation. Events were to disclose that Stalin never abandoned that plan at any time.

The American Communists, instructed by Moscow, kept this well in mind. They endlessly stated their determination, based on the Marxist-Leninist principle that all non-Soviet governments must be overthrown, that they would destroy the government of the United States. As late as 1936, in the midst of the United Front era, Earl Browder gave in a book, *What Is Communism?*, the details of how that destruction would be accomplished.

There was at least one agency of our government which understood that the Communist leopard had not changed its spots. That was the Federal Bureau of Investigation. The watch which the FBI kept on the Reds, even after Pearl Harbor, evoked bitter attacks from the Communist camp upon the Bureau and its chief, J. Edgar Hoover. William Z. Foster took the lead in this campaign by denouncing the FBI as "reactionary." The *Daily Worker* charged it with injuring the war effort. This became a stock argument of the Communists against anyone who sought to block the adoption of Soviet plans.

The Committee on Un-American Activities, then under the chairmanship of Representative Martin Dies, was also a target for the Red fusillade. While some questions may be raised as to whether Congressman Dies always chose his battleground with the greatest wisdom, he was only striving to do what would have saved this country a great tragedy from within. Dies was attempting to prevent Communists or their friends from getting into key government posts. And nothing, of course, could arouse the Red conspiracy more than that. They had seen the opportunity for them in the unguarded attitude of many of our American leaders and they would not be thwarted. They arranged that petition after petition signed by educators, scientists, publicists, social workers, clergymen, and other professional people flood Washington, demanding the end of the Dies Committee. On one occasion, no less than 1,250 eminent citizens, whose names are recorded in issue after issue of the *Daily Worker,* presented such a demand. While the committee was not abolished, this deluge of petitions to discredit it had a marked effect. The committee's work was slowed down and a doubt was created in every community as to the validity of its findings.

A distressing echo of all this survives today in a continued hesitancy to deal forthrightly and vigorously with the Communist fifth column. None of the eminent citizens who called for a halt to all investigation of Stalin's agents has ever apologized to the American people for thereby having made it possible for Alger Hiss to attain the high position he did in the State Department, and for his fellow Red infiltrators to penetrate equally high-level ranks in government and public opinion. While Browder was telling the American people in a radio broadcast that it was "the Communist Party policy . . . to subordinate our program of socialism" to the war effort, that conspiracy was officially cabling Stalin: "You have raised the glorious banner of Marx, Engels, and Lenin to new heights." In the Red Aesopian language, which was so well exposed in the trial of the eleven Communists in Foley Square as conspiratorial double-talk, "the banner of Marx, Engels, and Lenin" or Marxism-Leninism, is the commitment to Soviet world conquest. In praising Earl Browder's book, *Victory and After,* which was written to throw dust in the eyes of the American people, the *Daily Worker* explained Marxism-Leninism as "the world-wide revolutionary experience" and said that it was embodied in Browder's book. This was a tip-off to the comrades that, while Browder might speak softly here and there in his pages to win sorely needed American aid for Stalin, it was to be regarded as but a part of those flexible tactics to which the Red leaders repeatedly refer.

Of Communist tactics, espionage was the most dramatic feature, as revelations in recent years have shown. The voluntary admissions of Whittaker Chambers and Elizabeth Bentley which demonstrated that Red espionage rings had penetrated high into the State Department, the Treasury Department, and the Department of Commerce, were only a beginning of the story. In the very midst of the war, Dr. Clarence Hiskey, it was charged by witnesses who knew him, turned over notes on atomic bomb projects to "Arthur Adams," Soviet espionage agent. Hiskey had also endeavored to recruit John Hitchcock Chapin, a chemical engineer of the Chicago atomic project, as an espionage contact for Adams. Joseph Woodrow Weinberg, known for a time as "Scientist X," was detected in 1943 visiting the home of Steve Nelson, the Soviet espionage agent then in San Francisco. As a result of that meeting, Nelson was observed by government agents turning over secret information to Peter Ivanov, the Soviet Vice-Consul in San Francisco. Since Weinberg worked in the sensitive radiation laboratory of the University of California, the information passed on requires no explanation. That radiation laboratory was also penetrated, it has been charged, by Giovanni Rossi Lomanitz, the principal Communist Party organizer among the scientists there, and by David Bohm, engaged in especially secret laboratory work. Both Lomanitz and Bohm refused to answer questions as to their membership in the Communist Party or in the radiation laboratory cell.

Weinberg refused to state whether or not he knew Nelson, on the grounds that it would tend to incriminate him. But it is interesting to note that the third secretary of the Russian Embassy in Washington, Vassili M. Zubilin, made a special trip to San Francisco to pay Nelson in cash for services rendered. That meeting occurred in 1943, when Soviet Russia and the United States were supposedly allies. Five years later, when the Committee on Un-American Activities questioned the Soviet agent Nelson about his acquaintance with Zubilin, he gave the usual refusal to answer on the grounds that it would incriminate him. Since that time, although convicted, he has remained free to pursue his activities. These are samples, and only samples, of how our "gallant ally," whose honor was so high in the opinion of our statesmen, treated us. It treated us as a foe.

It may be recalled that in the case of the Rosenberg couple and Sobell, the first two of whom have been sentenced to death for Soviet atomic espionage, the argument which induced them to steal our secrets was that Soviet Russia was our ally and was being deprived by powerful interests in America of something it was entitled to have. It is precisely the same argument that was used to induce Dr. Richard Boyer, the Canadian scientist, and others in the Canadian ring, to turn over vital information to the Soviet agents.[3]

In its recent publication, *The Shameful Years*, presenting the record of Soviet espionage in the United

[3] These references to Soviet espionage, as all others to the same effect throughout this volume, are taken from the reports of the House Committee on Un-American Activities, the Canadian Royal Commission, and the proceedings of the Senate Subcommittee on Internal Security of the Committee on the Judiciary.

States, the House Committee on Un-American Activities has given a review of what happened during that time of pro-Soviet folly which began with Pearl Harbor. This report states:

Upon the entry of the United States into World War II it might have been assumed that the Soviet Union as an ally would discontinue its espionage activities within the United States. However, the opposite was the case. The Soviet Union intensified its espionage activities in this country.

The Committee report goes on to explain how this occurred.

The success of the Soviet espionage during this period may be attributed to a variety of circumstances. Principal among them was the fact that some Americans who, while not actual members of the Communist Party, but previously sympathetic to it, adopted the view that because the Soviets were allies, they should have access to any and all information and that they were merely facilitating the Soviets in making the information available.

It can readily be seen that such an attitude would be fostered by the friendly enthusiasm with which a great section of American officialdom received the Soviet "ally."

Something else also occurred to further this espionage, the sudden influx of Soviet subjects into this country to serve as employees of the various purchasing commissions and missions. On this matter the Committee comments, on the basis of data in its possession:

It has previously been shown that the Soviets had long utilized the Amtorg Trading Corp. as a cover for its espionage operations; however, with the opening of the immigration gates at the beginning of World War II, literally thousands of Russians entered the United States as employees of the Soviet Government Purchasing Commission. In addition to these, the Soviets increased and strengthened their espionage agents in the embassies and consulates.

In other words, while we were pouring out lend-lease to Soviet Russia, the Kremlin was pouring espionage agents into the United States, sometimes through the very agencies associated with lend-lease.

Infiltration of important posts in which government policy and public opinion could be influenced was regarded by the Soviet fifth column as even more valuable than espionage. It also provided sources of "information" in a natural way which amounted to espionage without the penalties attached to it.

Alger Hiss was held in high esteem by the Communist conspiracy not only because he stole valuable documents from the State Department, but also because he could persuade the United States and its leaders to give away great sections of the earth to Stalin. Hiss was the great hero at the United Nations Conference at San Francisco and its first General Secretary.

How much the American nation has suffered, and is still suffering, from the work of concealed Communists in key places is shown by the recent report of the McCarran Subcommittee of the Senate on infiltration in the telegraph industry. The press gave little notice to this startling story, which deeply affects American security at this present hour.

The challenging part of it is that J. I. Wilcox, Vice President of the Western Union Telegraph Company, admitted that members of the American Communications Association had free access to government wires, even those intended for military instructions. Joseph P. Selly, president of the ACA, also admitted that wires of the military establishment of the government and the

State Department passed through the hands of ACA members and could be examined by the shop stewards.

A situation more favorable to the Communist conspiracy could hardly be imagined—an assertion I make as an acknowledged former member of that conspiracy. The American Communications Association has a long record of following every delicate turn in the Communist line. In 1950 it was expelled from the Congress of Industrial Organizations on the grounds that it was Communist-controlled. Before the McCarran Subcommittee, its national officers refused to say whether they were members of the Communist Party or whether they knew any Communist leaders. They have all been identified before Senate or House committees as Communists.

The ACA has bargaining relations with the Western Union and other telegraph agencies in New York City, which give it virtual control of those facilities in the metropolis. The corporations excuse their recognition of this Communist-controlled group on the ground that it has so far been able to get the workers to vote for it as their bargaining agent. However, in numerous disputes with legitimate labor organizations, the corporations have sought to win public opinion against the union's contentions and have inserted large ads in the newspapers defending their case. Never, to my knowledge, have they done this when Communist control was actually involved.

What is even more serious than espionage in the vital telegraph and electric industries is the possibility that the Reds could shut them down by a general strike whenever it should serve Stalin's interests. The critical nature of this situation is intensified by the Kremlin's basic plan in case of war or attempted seizure of control in the United States. This has been written down repeatedly in official documents for the Communists to study and execute. It consists of the political strike, which is nothing other than bringing about widespread walkouts through demands for better wages and hours and then transforming these stoppages into movements to paralyze or overthrow the government.

This ACA case is an outstanding one in registering the bitter fruits of the years of folly. Many others could be recorded, including the rise in prestige of the Communist-controlled United Electrical, Radio, and Machine Workers Union through its participation with management in the "Nelson production committees." The effects of this infiltration will become clear as this account proceeds. It went far beyond labor. Congressional committee documents by the score tell us of the widening influence of the Communists and their friends during the World War II period in all classifications of professional life. In each case, it was a small but aggressive and secretly organized minority which spearheaded this advance of Red influence. As to the ACA, Communist control was dominant before World War II, but the war years gave it the opportunity to plant its feet more widely in the communications industry.

The process by which Communist participation in the war served as an explanation or excuse for cooperating with the Reds or their friends in front organizations is nowhere better illustrated than in the case of José Ferrer. This able and well-known actor received the Oscar award in 1951, despite considerable protest over his membership or sponsorship of Communist fronts. Under oath, before the House Committee on Un-American Activities, Ferrer gave in effect the Communist aim in the war as the reason for his becoming involved in a series of wider and wider fronts. To quote him: "The only time I could even remotely be said to have been in sympathy with any Communist aim was when it coincided with the aim of our government. For instance when they wanted to win the last war, I certainly was in sympathy with that. . . ." Accordingly, Ferrer became identified with the Artists Front To Win the War, well-known as a Communist front organized by John Howard Lawson, who later went to prison for the Communist cause and has been identified by many witnesses as the leading representative of the Communist Party in Hollywood. Ferrer then became associated with the American Committee for the Protection of the Foreign Born, notoriously subversive, as the Attorney General's list shows. He lent his name and help to the Joint Anti-Fascist Refugee Committee, which brought such leading Communists as Gerhart Eisler into the United States and other countries of the Western Hemisphere. He became head of the theater division of the Independent Committee of the Arts, Sciences, and Professions, the favorite creation of the Communists during the war period. Finally, after other such ventures, Ferrer was one of the prominent men and women who endorsed the candidacy of Benjamin J. Davis, Communist candidate for the New York City Council in 1945 and now one of the convicted eleven Red leaders.

A number of those who worked with or for the Communists in the professional ranks took advantage of the war to become connected with the Office of War Information and the Office of Strategic Services. For example, Leonard Bercovici, also known as Berkowitz, the motion picture writer who refused to answer questions about Communist affiliations before the House Committee, was with the OWI. Abraham Lincoln Polonsky, another screen and radio writer who refused to answer questions about Communists or the Communist Party, stated that he had been in secret work for the Office of Strategic Services during the war. Waldo Salt, likewise from Hollywood and the writing profession, even refused to state whether he knew J. Peters, the head of Red espionage in this country for the Communist International apparatus. Salt defied Congress on this and other matters connected with his alleged Red loyalty; he had been one of those to serve with the OWI during the war years.

Additional listings could be given of men with similar loyalties and similar background in trusted governmental posts. Those cited raise the curtain only slightly on the much wider scene of infiltration.

The years of folly are still marching along with us into 1952. The Communists and their fellow travelers are now taking advantage of the desire of all peoples, including our own, for peace in the same manner as they forwarded their goals through the American nation's desire to win the war. "The Pact of Peace," the Kremlin's chief present objective, includes those very things which will bring about surrender to Stalin. Pertinent to such a pact, as Moscow presents it, would be recognition of Red China and its seating in the United Nations; the ending of armaments for Japan and unification of Germany on the Soviet model; and other measures to disarm the United States in preparation for further Soviet aggression. These are the terms as set down in every Cominform demand.

To make this doubly clear, a special set of arguments has been furnished the Communists throughout the world under the title "Stalin on the War Danger and the Possibility of Averting It," translated in the theoretical organs of the Communist parties, including that of the

United States.[4] In typical Soviet fashion, the burden for aggression in Korea and elsewhere is placed on the shoulders of "the American imperialists." In contrast, the Soviet Union is declared, as usual, to be "the bulwark of peace, democracy, and socialism." Its conquest of China and most of Eastern Europe is described as "liberation."

Upon that distorted premise, this important directive to the Communists, while still affirming "the Marxist-Leninist position of the inevitability of war in the epoch of imperialism" tells us how "peace" can be won.

The Communist solution is a simple one, the complete victory of Soviet Russia. "One of the most important conditions for the prevention of a new world war and securing the preservation of peace," the aforementioned essay concludes, "is enhancement of the power of the Soviet Union which heads the mighty front of the fighters for peace, the multiplication of its economic successes, and the strengthening of its defensive capacity." With that must go the drawing away of the peoples of all countries from the United States and its "aggression" and "towards the Soviet Union, the bulwark of peace and security for all peoples."

So long as the Communists can still, seven years after the war, enlist prominent men and women behind such "peace" proposals, they are in a position still to confuse American public opinion. When a policy of appeasement still prevails, yielding to Soviet pressure in the name of peace rather than standing firmly against it in order to assure the end of World War III, the situation becomes more than critical. The Communists count on our weaknesses to continue hesitation and vacillation in the public mind and in official policy.

[4] This article of directives is published for the United States in *Political Affairs*, theoretical organ of the Communist Party, December, 1951.

# CHAPTER 2

# The Kremlin in the State Department

On October 12, 1942, in the midst of Stalin's golden harvest in influencing American opinion, the Communist leader Earl Browder went on a visit to Washington. It was a momentous trip, for Browder went there, in effect, as the ambassador of the Chinese Communists. Later, when his mission had been successfully completed, he described what had occurred as equivalent to "an agreement among nations." He had won the first round in what was to lead to the victory of Red China.

In Washington Browder, by personal and specific invitation, had a conference with Sumner Welles, then Under Secretary of State. He was accompanied by Robert Minor, Assistant Secretary of the Communist Party, and was introduced to Mr. Welles by Lauchlin Currie, Administrative Assistant to President Roosevelt. Currie has been mentioned prominently by Elizabeth Bentley as a friend and co-worker of the Soviet underground infiltration in Washington.

At this conference Mr. Welles assured Browder that the government of the United States "desires Chinese unity and deprecates civil strife in China." He stated that the United States would not favor Chiang Kai-shek against the Chinese Communists in order to aid "unity" in China. This decision, promptly communicated to the Chinese Communists, gave them a terrific boost.

Anyone in a high public position should have been aware of "the united front" tactic of the Communist conspiracy to win over and then destroy those with whom it co-operates. The State Department at that time, and Welles specifically, had at their disposal the open statement by George Dimitrov, General Secretary of the Communist International at its Seventh World Congress in 1935, defining the "united front" as a "Trojan horse policy." That stratagem was no secret. It had received extensive publicity throughout official circles in this country, and been particularly emphasized by the House Committee on Un-American Activities. The State Department could scarcely have failed to be aware of it. From that pronouncement, it should have recognized that any such pledge as the one Welles gave Browder must lead to a Communist victory in China. It is true, in possible explanation, that we were then at war with Japan and that "unity" in China would have helped defeat the Japanese. But the Communists made unity impossible. Chiang Kai-shek held off the Japanese, not in co-operation with the Communists, but in spite of the obstacles they put in his way. His success in this lonely struggle against our common enemy was greater than that of any of the weaker nations against the aggressor.

The news of Welles' concession to the Chinese Communists was emblazoned across the pages of the *Daily Worker* and spread far and wide throughout the country. The agreement gave the Chinese Communists enormous prestige. It was easy after that to campaign Americans into the belief that Mao Tse-tung and his followers were merely "agrarian reformers" and champions of "Asia for the Asiatics," not of Asia for Stalin. This Communist-launched campaign provided a springboard for the "coalition government" idea, adopted by the State Department, which was to lead to such tragedy in the Far East. The result, as we all know today, was Communist China—and Korea.

The Communists valued the Welles statement so highly that they accompanied its publication with a "retraction" by Browder of charges he had previously made that "reactionaries in the State Department" were injuring the Communists in China. It is a rare day, indeed, when any Communist leader will make a "retraction." In the published reports of the McCarran hearings, this unprecedented act is explained. Testimony before that Committee shows that the original "reactionaries in the State Department" charge by Browder on October 4, 1942, was made by prearrangement with Lauchlin Currie "in order to smoke out anti-Soviet elements in the State Department."

Since a Red China and a Red Poland were the first Soviet objectives, the October, 1942 Welles-Browder conference was a clear gain for Stalin. The planned conquests of China and Poland were necessary to the Kremlin's plans to check Japan from becoming a force that could halt Soviet advance in Asia and thereby pave the way for Eastern Europe to succumb to the fate of Poland.

The success of the Soviet fifth column, as early as 1942, with the United States State Department was a comparatively minor gain. For, as the record shows, from 1942 on the Kremlin worked best perhaps in our government's strategic departments. Campaigns initiated by Moscow and echoed by the Communist Party through the *Daily Worker* for certain policies and against certain personnel were almost miraculously achieved. This "golden" period of American adulation for our "allies" enabled men like Alger Hiss to get into positions where they could manipulate our policy in favor of Soviet Russia.

Stalin reaped the harvest from this infiltration in 1945 and 1946. Poland was handed over to Soviet domination with the full acquiescence and blessing of the United States. At the Yalta Conference on February 12, 1945, the United States agreed with Great Britain and Soviet Russia to the setting up of a "Polish Provisional Government of National Unity." This is what Stalin had wanted all along, since it was the "coalition government," or the "united front" idea, which had always been productive of Communist success. The very day before the Yalta agreement was signed, the Soviet radio gave notice that the Kremlin would use this agreement for its own purposes—by demanding the arrest of certain "traitors," all staunch opponents of Communist rule in Poland.

From that point the process of betrayal instigated by the agents and friends of the Soviet Union in the United States flourished. The Soviet armies came into complete control of Poland because of Stalin's betrayal in 1944 of the underground non-Communist Polish resistance to Hitler. The Polish underground, led by General Bor, and representing the vast majority of the Polish people, had armed in secret and prepared to strike against the Nazis at the proper hour. With the Soviet armies less than forty miles from Warsaw, the Soviet radio on July 29, 1944, called upon the armed underground in these words: "Poles, the time of liberation is at hand. Poles, to arms! There is not a moment to lose!" The people of Warsaw arose, only to be betrayed. For weeks the Soviet armies remained at approximately the same distance from Warsaw, permitting the Nazis to kill thousands of

Polish patriots and crush the uprising. Warsaw was left a shambles.

When the Yalta agreement was signed in 1945, the United States knew full well the extent of this perfidy, for our armed forces had sought in vain to parachute sufficient arms and supplies to the Poles to enable them to continue their resistance. Soviet Russia had coldly refused to allow American planes to land on Russian soil in the necessary shuttle trip from Great Britain.

This episode, well known in Washington, should have put American officials on guard against Soviet perfidy. And since Washington was well aware of these events, it makes what happened at Yalta all the more amazing.

After the Yalta agreement, Stalin proceeded, as could have been expected, to violate that pact. Washington was enormously co-operative in the matter. It sent Harry L. Hopkins to the Kremlin as spokesman for the American people. Hopkins was clearly a long-time apologist for Soviet Russia. He had even gone so far as to consult me, at that time a leading Communist, about Stalin's integrity. Hopkins broke the deadlock between the United States and Soviet Russia "by bowing to Russian pressure," as former Premier Stanislaw Mikolajczyk of Poland has so well put it. It was agreed that the Provisional Government of National Unity should come into existence only on condition that the Communists should have a decided majority in it. This sealed the fate of Poland. "The free and unfettered elections" mentioned in the Yalta Pact became a nightmare of terrorism against non-Communist Poles. Poland—overwhelmingly anti-Communist—fell under the heel of Stalin.[1]

---

[1] The story of Poland's betrayal, from which these references are drawn, has been told by Arthur Bliss Lane, our ex-Ambassador, in *I Saw Poland Betrayed*, and in Stanislaw Mikolajczyk's *The Rape of Poland*.

After the debacle in Poland the State Department tried to smooth things over with polite notes to the "Polish government." But it defined its position by refusing to bring the issue of Poland's betrayal to the floor of the United Nations, and finally climaxed the betrayal by admitting the new Communist Polish government into that body. The same series of incidents followed in the other countries of East Europe. In this connection, I remember clearly how, months before Yalta, when I was still a Communist, I was shown at our national headquarters in New York a map or plan presenting the exact division of Europe which took place during the two years following. I was told in confidence that the United States would agree to this division. That is substantially what occurred.

On his return from Moscow, Harry L. Hopkins represented his surrender to Stalin as a fulfillment of the Yalta agreement. The State Department accepted the Hopkins verdict. Dean Acheson had then become a power in the department, and his concurrence in the surrender of Poland was, as he has since made clear, even more than whole-hearted. His own law firm guaranteed the foundation of the new Communist government by obtaining immediate American loans to Poland of ninety million dollars. With such initial co-operation on the part of the United States, what was there to delay Stalin in snatching off Bulgaria, Rumania, Hungary, Albania, Czechoslovakia, Latvia, Esthonia, Lithuania—all of which was accomplished without any effective protest from our State Department?

Meanwhile, the American Communists had a more difficult task assigned them by Moscow—obtaining American agreement to a Red China. The United States had always stood for the Open-Door policy in China, and it was the United States alone which had finally defeated Japan. Therefore, the discussions in the American Politburo made clear that it would be harder to persuade the American public to accept the Communist conquest of China than of Eastern Europe. Stalin had long ago declared that a Soviet China would be the springboard to world-wide aggression. In pursuance of their leader's announced aim, the American Communists launched a persistent campaign to rid the State Department of every official who might offer any opposition to Soviet plans in the Far East. The first man against whom this campaign was directed was Adolf A. Berle, Assistant Secretary of State. As early as October 4, 1942, the Communists assailed him as "the sinister A. A. Berle, champion of Munich, anti-Soviet intriguer in our State Department." They continued to work for the displacement of Berle until 1944, when success crowned their efforts.

The Communists had already been greatly encouraged in March, 1943, when Sumner Welles, speaking for the State Department, rebuked our Ambassador to Soviet Russia, Admiral William H. Standley, for reminding the Soviet dictatorship that it was not adequately informing the Russian people of the aid they were receiving from the United States. In a notable press conference Welles repudiated our Ambassador to Moscow, declaring the statement had been made without consultation with Washington, and that no doubt of any kind should be cast upon the "trust and understanding" between the United States and the Soviet dictatorship.

The Communists opened fire on Standley in an attack lasting a number of days and which they arrogantly declared was directed at "others in the State Department who should be given a chance to spend all their time playing golf and attending fashionable cocktail parties."

Their demand that Standley should "go back on the retired list" was speedily put into effect by the State Department.

In the drive against Standley and all other officials who were aware of Soviet designs, the Communists circulated widely an address made at that time by Vice President Henry A. Wallace at Delaware, Ohio, in which he said that the great danger to future peace lay in our "double-crossing of Russia." The Vice President placed the whole burden of international peace on the United States. He was greatly aided by Wendell Willkie, who naïvely declared that Standley had not been "wise or correct."

After Standley's removal, it was clear that no even moderately ambitious officer in the State Department would henceforth dare take an analytical or critical view of Soviet purposes. Furthermore, it became for such employees really dangerous to assume anything but an all-out position in favor of Soviet designs in the Far East.

The next target in the Communist campaign for a Soviet China was Joseph C. Grew, Under Secretary of State in charge of Far Eastern Affairs. On June 2, 1945, the Politburo of the American Communists, preparing for the cold war against the United States, declared that one big item in its program was to "curb those who seek American imperialist control in the Far East." The opposite of "American imperialist control" they defined as "coalition government" in China and American military aid to the Chinese Reds. As Mr. Grew could not agree to anything of the sort, the Communists and their friends decided that he must go.

Mr. Grew offended the Communists on another point upon which they were determined: "A tough peace for Japan." In the case of Germany, they had succeeded, through Harry Dexter White, an important agent of theirs in the post of Under Secretary of the Treasury, to prepare and get accepted the Morgenthau Plan, which would have prostrated the German nation. The mischief that this plan caused to American interests and security in Germany cannot be overestimated. That was its purpose. With the same goal in mind in the Far East—to alienate Japan from the United States by harsh treatment and thereby throw that country into the arms of of Soviet Russia—the Communists fought for a Morgenthau Plan for the defeated Japanese Empire.

On July 24, 1945, the Communists opened up their guns on Grew in a leading editorial in the *Daily Worker* entitled: "Mr. Grew Must Explain." It demanded that the State Department apply terms of "unconditional surrender" to Japan. Since the *Daily Worker* is not a daily paper in the normal sense of the word, but a telegraph agency of directives to the conspirators, the Communists speeded this attack on Grew throughout the country. They spread it into non-Communist organizations. During August, the Communists carried on a continual barrage against Grew, representing him to be against the Chinese Communists and to be acting for "capitalist forces" favorable to reaction in Japan. They linked his name with that of Ambassador Patrick Hurley and Lieutenant General Albert Wedemeyer as men who should be replaced. By August 14, V-J Day, they charged that Hurley and Wedemeyer "were promoting civil war in China" by not siding with the Chinese Reds. In conclusion they demanded in a leading editorial in the *Daily Worker:* "The State Department should be bombarded with messages demanding the recall of Ambassador Hurley and General Wedemeyer, and the immediate cleansing of the people in the State Department responsible for this suicidal policy."

By August 17, in a miraculously short time, Grew had retired from his post. His place was taken by Dean Acheson, who as early as 1944 had been labeled by the Communists as one of the most "forward-looking men" in the State Department. Not yet fully satisfied, the Communists insisted that Grew "must really be retired from public life and in no case appointed to any post dealing with Far Eastern affairs." They frankly stated their reason for this ultimatum, given as though from one great power to another. It was that Joseph C. Grew had been "long a foe of Chinese unity." By "unity" they meant a complete Communist victory.

Fearful lest Grew find a way back into the State Department, the Reds kept up their assault, berating him for having filed charges against John Stewart Service, who had been detected by the FBI giving top-secret State Department documents to Philip Jaffe, now established by testimony as a Soviet espionage agent. The reinstatement of Service by the State Department two days after Grew went out was another triumph for the Communists. The *Daily Worker* chortled with joy when the State Department reinstated him.

Some of the cause for their joy can be gauged by the *Daily Worker* statement on November 28, 1945, when the Communist campaign against Major General Patrick Hurley led to his resignation as our Ambassador to China. It wrote:

It is well known that liberal elements like John Carter Vincent and John S. Service in the State Department have opposed Hurley's reappointment. The former ambassador continually sought to by-pass them in his one-man rule of the embassy in China.

It is a significant reflection of his mentality that all his critics are called Communists, and his main fire was centered on 'the considerable section of our State Department which is endeavoring to support Communism generally as well as specifically in China.'

That the men who opposed Hurley thereby helped Communism is now a matter of record. The Communists had carried their attack on him down to the very day of his resignation and even thereafter. Their indictment of Hurley in itself proves this. For they charged:

In China, Hurley's flamboyant, self-advertising methods were notorious; he was strongly attracted to Chiang Kai-shek for he recognized the man who might build a reactionary China subservient to a strong, imperialist America—at the expense of the Soviet Union and Great Britain as well.

Such words, unadorned by their Communist window-dressing, mean simply that Hurley was seeking to defend American interests and American security in the Far East. The Communists wanted to bring about what has now occurred—victory for Soviet aggression.

Another victim of the Communist campaign was Eugene C. Dooman, who until 1945 was for several years head of the Far Eastern Division of the State Department. Dooman angered Stalin's agents by opposing a hard peace for Japan and favoring a policy of occupation such as was carried out so successfully by General Douglas MacArthur. He was soon removed from his post, and, to the great pleasure of the Communists, succeeded by John Carter Vincent, who with Owen Lattimore accompanied Vice President Henry Wallace on his trip to China and Soviet Siberia in 1944. On that trip Vincent and Lattimore were together warmly toasted by Sergei Goglidze, chief of the Siberian slave-labor camps, as those "on whom rests the responsibility for the future of

China." [2] Vincent was widely known as favoring a tough peace with Japan, and therefore filled the Communist formula of the kind of man to have, in 1945, as head of the State Department's Far Eastern Division.

The Communist conspiracy was also author of the cry, "MacArthur must go," raised in that strategic year of 1945. As editor of the Communist daily paper, I was present at the discussions in which the campaign was hatched against the Supreme Commander in the Pacific. In my presence, illegal aliens in the service of Stalin, subjects of Soviet Russia such as Alexander Bittelman and Robert William Weiner, both leaders in the Red conspiracy here, laid the foundations for slanderous assaults on the hero of the Pacific war. Meeting on the ninth floor of 35 East 12th Street in New York City, the national headquarters of the Communist Party, they ordered a ruthless drive for the removal of General MacArthur. This drive was to reach a high point on September 22, 1945, when the *Daily Worker* editorially (I was still its editor at that time) declared the General "unfit" for the crucially important assignment of shaping the future of Japan.

On the previous day, the Communist paper had told its readers why MacArthur was "unfit" in its eyes. The Reds feared that he would build up Japan into a "possible bulwark against the Soviet Union and the progressive forces in Asia," that is, he would make sure that there would be no Soviet conquest of Asia. This openly expressed concern, appearing in the columns of the *Daily Worker,* was based upon the belief that MacArthur's continued presence in Japan would influence events in China against the Communists and might also influence

[2] This episode is mentioned by Henry A. Wallace in his *Soviet Asia Mission,* 1944.

American policy. It was generally recognized that the Pacific commander was an intense and intelligent opponent of Soviet designs, particularly in the Far East.

We have an interesting footnote to this Red concern about MacArthur, in the revelations of Major General Frank Lowe, on January 25, 1952, to a staff writer of the Scripps-Howard press. General Lowe was the personal representative of President Truman in Korea, and now charges that cables to the President in regard to MacArthur were never delivered to Mr. Truman. They were intercepted by those who wanted to destroy MacArthur, Lowe states. In that connection, Jim Lucas, the Scripps-Howard writer who obtained the interview, made the following allegations:

The State Department, which he [General Lowe] charged, has been guilty of "daily appeasement of the Communists in Asia," feared and hated General MacArthur "because he was right and it was wrong" and was set on undermining him because he was determined "to meet the issue head on."

"There is no such a thing as half a war and there never will be," Gen. Lowe said. "The State Department wanted him to fight a commissar war. It tried to make his decisions for him. One by one we are doing the things Douglas MacArthur told us we would have to do.

"But I am afraid we have missed the boat. In April we could have destroyed the Chinese Communist armies in Korea. Instead, we've given them seven months in which to build up their strength. It will be much harder now."

If President Truman's former personal representative is correct in these claims, then the appeasement attitude which surrendered so much of the Far East to Stalin and unseated MacArthur has led us to a virtual defeat in Korea. What is more serious is that the defeat was totally unnecessary and could instead have been a victory.

General MacArthur's additional offense was that he also was opposed to a hard peace for Japan. In their efforts to win such a peace, the Communists represented the chief enemies of a free Japan to be the Zaibatsu, or industrialists, and the sole "democrats" to be the Communists and concealed Communists here. The Reds distributed thousands of copies of a statement of September 4, 1945, by Owen Lattimore echoing the Stalinist attack on the Zaibatsu. A special order went out from the party leadership for the distribution of Lattimore's statement to every possible trade union, civic group, and professional organization which the Reds could penetrate.

The anti-MacArthur propaganda, hatched by the comrades, presented him, of course, as a tool of the Zaibatsu. It sank to the usual Communist depths of character assassination with a special series of articles from the Philippine Communist Party in the *Daily Worker* of mid-September. These articles, which were a potpourri of all the slander that could be organized against MacArthur, pictured him as an agent of the "Fascists" in the Philippines and in all Asia. The series was obtained from the Huks (the Philippine Communists), by James Allen, a former Comintern representative in these islands. Allen was one of the open Communists whose name was added to the contributors of *Pacific Affairs,* the organ of the Institute of Pacific Relations, while Owen Lattimore was its editor. Allen appears prominently in the records of the McCarran Committee as an infiltrator into the IPR and as a Soviet agent.

New encouragement was given to the Reds when Dean Acheson, then Acting Secretary of State, delivered on September 19, 1945, what the *Daily Worker* exultantly called a "sharp rebuke to the flamboyant General." This was three days after the last of the scurrilous articles against

MacArthur had appeared in the Red paper. Acheson's "rebuke" was on behalf of the hard peace for which the Reds were battling and was issued because General Mac-Arthur dared to suggest that things were going so well in Japan that a much reduced Army of Occupation could be considered within the next six months. Editorially, the *Daily Worker* backed Acheson wholeheartedly and advised President Truman to follow his instructions.

On September 26, the *Daily Worker* declared editorially: "It is time to crack down on MacArthur." At the same time, Frederick Vanderbilt Field, now definitely proven a Communist agent actively engaged in the infiltration of the Institute of Pacific Relations, called upon the comrades to combine their attacks on "MacArthur's outrage in Japan" with a national fight to get the White House completely behind the Chinese Communists.

Throughout 1946, as an illustration, MacArthur was under continuous and bitter attack from Tass, the Soviet news agency, echoed by the *Daily Worker*. The objectives of this campaign were to prevent that successful administration in Japan which MacArthur fortunately attained, to open the way for such chaotic conditions in Korea as would make what has since happened possible, and to bring about a Communist victory in China. On New Year's Day, 1946, the *Daily Worker* published a special editorial declaring "MacArthur Unfit for Tokyo Post." Of the General they wrote: "He behaves like a sovereign power, as though Japan were one of his Philippine plantations." They stated that "MacArthur must go if the United States intends to have this Allied Council accomplish anything." For aid in their plan to oust MacArthur, the Communists again looked to the State Department. "Back in September, the State Department told Mac-Arthur where to get off on that business of how long the occupation of Japan would last. Why don't they speak up now?"

The prestige of General MacArthur, as the hero of the Pacific War and because of his able administration in Japan, almost the only bright spot in the record of American foreign affairs since World War II, prevented the Reds in 1945 and for over five years afterward from achieving their aim to discredit and oust him. But they kept up a relentless battle against him, stimulated by Soviet Russia's charge that he was "outmoded" in Japan. Nothing could exceed the joy of the *Daily Worker* when at long last, in 1951, the Red objective was finally gained and the man whom they looked upon as their most formidable opponent in the Far East was removed from the scene.

The Reds continually compared MacArthur to General Patrick Hurley, for whose resignation as Ambassador to China they had so successfully campaigned. Hurley was accused not only of ignoring the "career men" in the State Department, such as John Carter Vincent and John Stewart Service, but also of showing contempt for the recommendations of the "Far Eastern experts" who had so aggressively forwarded the idea that the Chinese Communists were not Communists in the strict sense and were not bound to Moscow. The *Daily Worker* specifically mentioned that Hurley's lack of knowledge about China was indicated in his attitude toward Israel Epstein, whom it represented as a high authority on Chinese affairs. In 1951, a number of witnesses testifying before the McCarran Committee established that Epstein, an alien, was a Communist of high standing and a Soviet espionage agent.

It was the Epstein advice on China, favoring the Communist, and not the Hurley, view of strengthening

Chiang Kai-shek as our ally, that the State Department adopted. That led to a sharp-worded ultimatum to Chiang Kai-shek that he must accept the idea of coalition government with the Communists if he were to have American sympathy.

The concept of "coalition government," which the Communists had originated, was based on the portrayal of the Chinese Reds as "agrarian reformers" and as proponents of an "Asia for the Asiatics" policy. This implied to the Western World that they would not follow the Kremlin and would not advance Stalin's rule in Asia. An entire school of writers arose, with Epstein as a conspicuous example, to deceive the American people with this false picture. These writers, working with and through the Institute of Pacific Relations, helped to ease the road for Communist influences in the State Department to hand China over to Stalin.

Within the Communist Party, this tactic was first brought forward by Earl Browder in a secret conference in 1937, attended by Frederick Vanderbilt Field of the Institute of Pacific Relations. Browder stated that the old line of talk that the Chinese Communists were seeking to sovietize China was to be abandoned. In its place, the Communists at work within the Institute of Pacific Relations, and elsewhere in concealed positions, were to present the Chinese Reds as purely agrarian reformers.

This scheme came to full fruition in 1944 and 1945 when publishers were deluged with books and magazines with articles extolling the "democratic Chinese agrarian reformers." One of the "experts" who carried on this work was Maxwell L. Stewart, editor of the Public Affairs Pamphlets, and closely connected with the IPR. In a pamphlet prepared for the Institute in 1944, entitled *Wartime China,* Mr. Stewart wrote:

As China is not like any other country, so Chinese Communism has no parallel elsewhere. You can find in it resemblances to Communist movements in other countries and you can also find resemblances to the 'grass roots' Populist movements that have figured in American history. Because there is no other effective opposition party in China, the Communists have attracted the support of many progressive and patriotic Chinese who know little of the doctrines of Karl Marx or Stalin and care less. Raymond Gram Swing described Chinese Communists as "agrarian radicals trying to establish democratic practices."

As late as March, 1950, Owen Lattimore followed up this distortion of the Communist Chinese by his contribution in the *United Nations World,* entitled "Asia Reconquers Asia." He wrote:

It is clear that the change of power in China cannot properly be described as primarily a victory either of Communist armies or of Communist ideas. The chief phenomenon has been the moral and political background of the National Government of China, whose "ability" to collapse greatly exceeded the ability of the Communists to push it over.

That the State Department, with the aid of Lattimore and others of similar views, was decisive in this "pushing over" of Chiang Kai-shek's government is carefully omitted in the *United Nations World* article. This began with our government's gift of Manchuria to Stalin, which took from Chiang Kai-shek vast and essential sources of industrial and military supplies. It was initiated by our State Department, though Soviet Russia had taken no part in the war against Japan. Wishing to continue the illusion that Red China had no close bonds with Soviet Russia, Lattimore added:

It is also clear that Russian intervention, in the way of supplying either munitions or political and military advisers, was insignificant. The importance of this relative absence of Russian intervention in China has been overlooked partly because of the human tendency of wishful thinking.

What this "foremost American expert on Far Eastern affairs," as the *United Nations World* described him, wants us to believe is that there has been "the rise of an Asia which cannot be controlled either from the West or from Soviet Russia."

As a professor reputedly familiar with Far Eastern documents, Lattimore must know of the close connection between the Chinese Communists and the Kremlin. It appears in the proceedings of the Seventh World Congress of the Communist International, in the official declarations of the Chinese Communist Party, and in the current organs of the Cominform. It is based upon the recognition by the Chinese Communist Party that Stalin is "the leader and teacher of the toilers of the world."

Since Lattimore was an important adviser to the State Department, his words are of great value in throwing light on what happened in Asia. His views dominate the White Paper on China, prepared by Dr. Philip Jessup, which in effect is based on the premise that a Red China was inevitable and that any State Department acts which helped advance that development were necessary, if not all to the good.

Another agency operating on the State Department was the *United Nations World,* whose editor, from 1946 to 1950, was Louis Dolivet, a veteran Soviet agent in Europe. Dolivet has been definitely identified as a Communist who concealed his affiliations while in the United States. He was an active participant in the Institute of Pacific Relations.

Another writer who played a big part in misrepresenting the Chinese Reds to Americans was Edgar Snow, author of *Red Star Over China* and for a number of years on the editorial board of the *Saturday Evening Post*. Perhaps the most indicative statement about Snow was made in a review in *Pacific Affairs* of a book by his wife, Nym Wales, *Inside Red China*. The IPR magazine, with Lattimore as its editor, declared:

It is curious how much of their good reputation abroad the Chinese Communists owe to one man—Edgar Snow. . . . Nym Wales, as the wife of Edgar Snow, will inevitably have her work compared with that of her famous husband. . . . She is not impartial, she thoroughly approves of the Chinese Communists . . . so she writes with gay excitement and eager partisanship.

Both of the Snows have been identified before the McCarran Subcommittee as Communists.

The *Daily Worker* repeatedly, of course, paid tribute during the war and post-war years to these writers on the Far East who were deceiving Americans as to the nature of the Reds in China. Joseph Starobin, its foreign editor, took occasion in a review he wrote of Philip Jaffe's *New Frontiers in Asia,* to praise these writers. Jaffe, it should be recalled, is the Soviet agent who accompanied Lattimore on a special trip to the Red-ruled provinces of China in 1937 and who directed the stealing of 1700 confidential documents from the State Department and other American government agencies in the *Amerasia* case.

Of the writers applauded by the Communists Starobin wrote:

Militarists like Patrick J. Hurley are riled by the virtual unanimity of American intellectual opinion on the broad issues of the future of Asia. The writers, experts, journalists

—even career diplomats in the State Department—are almost unanimous in their judgment of the reactionary character of the Kuomintang leaders, in their sympathy for the Chinese Communist program, and their emphasis on the need of an independent, democratic India. There is probably no other phase of American policy on which there is such a broad agreement among well-informed people. This has given rise to a virtual renaissance of American writing and thinking on the Far East.

He went on to heap praise upon Owen Lattimore, Kate Mitchell, Lawrence K. Rosinger, Andrew Roth, Harrison Forman, and Gunther Stein.

All of these writers have been identified under oath as Communists, with the exception of Harrison Forman. Testimony concerning him reveals his close connection with the Communists and his agreement that they should put all pressure behind the promotion of his book. The list of pro-Chinese Communist authors approved by the *Daily Worker* included, among others, Richard Lauterbach, Theodore White, Annalee Jacoby, and Jack Belden.

The "career men" in the State Department, headed by Alger Hiss, and the pro-Communist writers, headed by Owen Lattimore, were among the chief agents in bringing about the havoc in Europe and Asia which confronts the United States today. As a result of their recommendations, our government consented to the absurd Red corridor around Berlin, which cost us so heavily in the airlift, and incidentally diverted our energies and attention while the Kremlin took over China. Their advice also produced the unfortunate Italian treaty whereby a major part of the Italian navy was turned over to Moscow and a substantial delivery of Italian finished products stipulated for delivery to the Soviet government. These were harsh terms to impose upon a defeated and impoverished country, and Communist agitation within Italy took immediate advantage of the consequent difficulties of the Italian people to lay the blame at the door of "American imperialism." Our present costly efforts to "stop" Communism in Italy are thus made more difficult by this shortsighted policy. In late 1951, efforts were made to repair the damage done in Italy by a proposal to revise the treaty. But the initial advantage gained by the Communists still raised a question, in the minds of many Italians, as to what the future would bring.

The large immediate conquests achieved so easily by the Kremlin in China and Poland gave an impetus to the events which led to the disaster in Korea, and to the taking over by the Kremlin of Hungary, Bulgaria, and Rumania. Although the peoples of these countries, as especially evidenced in the huge anti-Communist vote in Hungary in 1945, indicated that Stalin had not quite completed his tyranny, our State Department did nothing. Except in the half-hearted move in Korea, the United Nations was not even called upon to defend the rights of the subjugated nations. It is natural to conclude that this was a continuation of the policy that had sacrificed China and Poland. As to the one place where Soviet aggression finally had been challenged—in the military report of the New York *Times*—its author, Hanson W. Baldwin, admitted on January 3, 1952: "The United States political and military position in Korea has become worse instead of better in the seven months since the cease-fire talks started. The reduction in military pressure on the enemy, plus extensive Russian material help, has enabled the Communists to increase their air and ground strength and to build up supplies." That state-of-affairs is the logical development not only of the whole appeasement policy that made possible the Korean conflict by building up Red China; it is also the sad result of rejecting the advice of General Douglas MacArthur on the conduct of the Korean war, a rejection which flowed naturally from previous State Department policies.

In 1951, the Communists conducted a series of celebrations for their victories in the various nations under satellite regimes. In each instance, whether it was in China or in Poland, Red gains were depicted as defeats for the "imperialists" and "warmongers" of the United States. These gains were represented as prefiguring the downfall of the United States.

The record shows that these defeats for our country were overwhelmingly the fruit of Red infiltration in the State Department and of Red influences operating effectively within that department. Not the least of these influences was the Communist control of the Institute of Pacific Relations. A review of that unique organization, its history, and the measures it took to assure the adoption of Communist views in Washington is a most revealing chapter in the present study.

# CHAPTER 3

# The Institute of Pacific Relations

In the Communist penetration of the State Department, the Institute of Pacific Relations was undoubtedly of decisive importance. This organization, as defined by Edward C. Carter, a former president of the American branch, is a "loose federation of some ten or twelve national institutes devoted to the study of the problems of the Pacific—economic, social, political, and so on." These national institutes were supposedly composed of public-spirited citizens, statesmen, and publicists from the various nations interested in the Pacific area. The American section has been typical of those associations in this country dedicated to a kindly purpose, which the Communists, with their discipline and concealment, could easily infiltrate. The record shows that in the case of the IPR they proceeded successfully to do so.[1]

It was perfectly natural that the IPR should establish relations with key figures in the State Department. As for

[1] All the data in this chapter have been taken from the proceedings of the Subcommittee on Internal Security of the Senate Committee on the Judiciary, Pat McCarran, chairman, and from the report of the House Committee on Un-American Activities Committee on the Richard Sorge spy ring.

its purposes, however, nothing perhaps indicates more clearly what the American IPR was after than the strenuous, although "confidential," efforts of E. C. Carter to get General George Marshall, then Secretary of State, and other leading men in Washington to give their attention to *The Unfinished Revolution in China* by Israel Epstein. This was a definite plea for the Chinese Communists and, ultimately, a Red government for China. For Epstein was a Soviet espionage agent, whom the Communists had imported into the United States from England, and his book had received laudatory reviews in the New York *Times* by Owen Lattimore (June 22, 1947) and in the Communist paper, the *New Masses* by Frederick Vanderbilt Field, then a member of the IPR's executive committee and openly a Communist. Two years earlier, Field had covered the San Francisco meeting of the United Nations for the *Daily Worker,* which played up his official connection with the American IPR. A pamphlet he wrote at that time, published by the Communists through their Workers, Library Publishers, championing the Communist line on the Far East, was widely circulated among influential non-Communist groups carrying special weight because of his prestige as an IPR executive. When Frederick Vanderbilt Field was finally jailed in 1951 for contempt of court in refusing to give the names of those who contributed to the bail bonds of the Communist-dominated Civil Rights Congress, it became common knowledge that he had long been a leading agent of the pro-Chinese Communist conspiracy in this country. Under the name of Spencer he had, in the early thirties, published a magazine, *China Today,* which openly championed the Chinese Reds. His co-worker in that enterprise was Philip Jaffe, subsequently identified as a Soviet espionage agent, who functioned at that time under the alias of Phillips. In 1937, with Jaffe and Owen Lattimore, Field founded *Amerasia,* a successor to *China Today* and heir to its subscription lists.

But all this was not so clear in the thirties as it is now. And nothing could have served Soviet designs better in that decade than for Frederick Vanderbilt Field, a man of wealth and family, to hold the title of Executive Secretary of the American IPR. By 1934, Field had acquired that post, and he left it only to become in 1939 the directing executive of the American Peace Mobilization, an open Communist front formed to oppose Roosevelt's policy of aid to Britain and champion the Hitler-Stalin pact during the period of that pact's existence. It was under Field's direction that the APM picketed the White House in an attack on British aid, thus stimulating the strikes that so crippled our defense production in that critical period. Correspondence from the IPR files, now made public by the McCarran Subcommittee, reveals that Dr. Philip Jessup, currently American ambassador-at-large by Presidential appointment, sought to persuade Field to remain with the IPR. This though he knew of Field's affiliation with the patently Communist-inspired American Peace Mobilization. When Field, under Politburo orders, insisted upon leaving, Jessup still expressed the hope that the retiring secretary would be of service to the IPR. Field continued as a member of the Executive Committee until 1948.

One of Field's assets to the American IPR was his ability and willingness to meet some of its deficits from time to time. While the officials of the organization have admitted to contributions from him in the neighborhood of $60,000, larger sums have been hinted at. The American IPR did receive, it is true, a few substantial grants from foundation funds for special research. But since

Field's aid helped maintain the permanent staff, it was more important than the figures might indicate.

When the setup of the American section of the IPR is understood, the ease with which the Communist design was accomplished will be appreciated. Though leading industrialists, lawyers, and educators innocently lent their names to the IPR, the executive staff was a dominant factor in policies and practices. This is a normal procedure in many organizations of this type. In the case of the American section, the staff was clearly pro-Soviet, and it worked to obtain favorable American attitudes toward the Chinese Communists. Aside from Field, an important figure was Owen Lattimore, who from 1934 to 1941 was editor of *Pacific Affairs,* one of the organs of the IPR. Lattimore worked closely with Field both on this publication and on *Amerasia.* Most of the other staff members, such as Harriet Lucy Moore, identified by several witnesses as an active Communist and whose writings show a clear pro-Soviet slant, were of a like character.

In 1941, the IPR received a grant of $90,000 from the Carnegie and Rockefeller foundations for research on Pacific affairs and relations. The Chinese end of this study was assigned by E. C. Carter to Chao-ting Chi, Asiaticus, and Chen Han-seng. All three were Communists, Chi was open in his affiliations, and, as far back as December, 1925 had written in the *Workers Monthly,* then the organ of the Workers Communist Party of America: "The world of imperialism is passing. Let us join hands with all enemies of imperialism, disregarding race, creed, or nationality." That statement was specifically aimed at soliciting support for the "first Negro Workers Congress." Asiaticus was a German Communist, a protégé of Gerhart Eisler. His real name was Heinz

Müller. He had, on orders from the Communist International, worked in China on behalf of the Kremlin. He had written articles for the Soviet official newspaper, *Izvestia,* in 1937. Lattimore was aware of this in 1938, according to the testimony of Dr. Karl Wittfogel, former German Communist, now a professor in this country and an authority on China, who himself advised Lattimore of the Communist official connections and duties of Asiaticus.

It is informative to learn, therefore, that Lattimore wrote to Carter on July 10, 1938: "I think that you are pretty cagey in turning over so much of the China section of the inquiry to Asiaticus, Han-seng, and Chi," and made himself clear by stating: "They will bring out the absolutely essential radical aspects but can be depended on to do it with the right touch."

That was not all. Continuing, Lattimore wrote: "For the general purposes of this inquiry, it seems to me that the good scoring position, for the IPR, differs with different countries. For China my hunch is that it will pay to keep behind the official Chinese Communist position—far enough not to be covered by the same label—but enough ahead of the active Chinese liberals to be noticeable." Of the attitude to be adopted toward the Soviet Union he added: "For the USSR—back their international policy in general, but without using their slogans and above all without giving them or anybody else an impression of subservience."

It was this covert but definite method of getting over his pro-Soviet ideas that led Alexander G. Barmine, former Soviet General in the Red Army Intelligence, to designate Lattimore as "the smoothest propagandist among them all [meaning the score of writers favoring Red China and Soviet aspirations in the Far East] precisely because he gives the appearance of being objective, realistic, and factual." Barmine delivered this verdict on Lattimore in reviewing his *Solution in Asia,* which is a skillful championship of the Chinese Communists and of Soviet Russia. The blurb writer for the jacket of Lattimore's book, as Barmine pointed out, "spilled the beans" when he described the Lattimore work:

He [Lattimore] shows that all the Asiatic peoples are more interested in actual democratic practices, such as the one they can see in action across the Russian border, than they are in the fine theories of Anglo-Saxon democracies which come coupled with ruthless imperialism. . . . He inclined to support American newspapermen who report that the only real democracy in China is found in Communist areas.

In the same work, Lattimore represented the Soviet dictatorship as appearing in the eyes of the Asiatic peoples as follows: "The Soviet Union stands for strategic security, economic prosperity, technological progress, miraculous medicine, free education, equality of opportunity, and democracy; a powerful combination."

The man who held these views, and who played so large a part in the Institute of Pacific Relations, was no ordinary citizen. He had accompanied Vice President Henry A. Wallace on his mission in 1944 to Soviet Asia and China. Of him Mr. Wallace had written: "On my mission in China I was fortunate to have along an adviser who had served in 1942–43 as President Roosevelt's personal envoy to Chiang Kai-shek. He was Owen Lattimore, a statesman in Pacific affairs and a scholar in the Chinese language." So well did the former Vice President think of Lattimore that he mentioned him twenty-one times in a comparatively short book.

Moreover, it was Lattimore, acting as an adviser to the

State Department, who recommended in 1949 that the United States withdraw from Korea, omit Japan as a possible major ally, hurry recognition of Communist China, and keep away from all "local entanglements" which would irritate Soviet Russia. This secret report was brought out through Senator Joseph R. McCarthy's charges in 1950. It was a recommendation of complete retreat and surrender to the Soviet regime in the Far East. According to former Governor Harold Stassen of Minnesota, Lattimore dominated the confidential conference of "experts" called by the State Department in 1949, which urged recognition of Communist China and other major steps helpful to Stalin's advance in Asia. According to Mr. Stassen, among these steps were the breaking of the Nationalist blockade of the China coast, American intervention in favor of the Communists, and the feebly hopeful view that Soviet Communism was "not as aggressive" as Hitler. Professor Kenneth Colgrove of Northwestern University, who had formerly been rather closely identified with Lattimore, confirmed the Stassen statements.

Mr. Stassen declared that he opposed each point of the Lattimore proposals and finally appealed to Philip Jessup not to agree with the recommendations or to follow them. According to Stassen, Jessup's answer was that "the greater logic" was with the Lattimore view.

Lattimore denied these allegations, releasing in support of his statements extracts from his remarks. These clearly suggested the recognition of Communist China and the abandonment of Korea as "an extremely unsavory police state." Mr. Lattimore said:

Couldn't we consider the desirability of an American approach to the problem of recognizing the new regime as well as this particular problem. . . . Couldn't we couple recognizing the new regime in China with a number of positive steps in China, showing American initiative and desire to get things done in the improvement of various situations. . . .

But these proposals, coupled with those of others in the "Lattimore group" made public by Stassen, involved the surrender of the Chinese people to Stalin, which the Communist leaders since Lenin have declared to be the jumping-off place for the conquest of Asia and the world. As a sample of other proposals made by those close to Lattimore, Ben Kizer, active in the Institute of Pacific Relations in the Northwest, suggested that the United States government prompt Great Britain to recognize the Red regime of Mao Tse-tung.

Lattimore's encouragement of recognition of Red China was in no way at variance with his favorable reports on Soviet Russia and the Chinese Communists, which won him honorable mention in the *Daily Worker* a few years before. It can also be recalled that when he served as editor of *Pacific Affairs* in the thirties, Lattimore introduced a number of Communists and pro-Communists into its pages as contributors. Among these was James S. Allen, identified by Hede Massing as Sol Auerbach, who was for a time Communist International representative in the Philippines and later foreign editor of the *Daily Worker*. There was also Abraham Chapman, known as John Arnold, who was one of the chief editorial writers for *Freiheit,* Communist New York Yiddish-language paper.

When Lattimore appeared before the McCarran Subcommittee in early 1952, he assailed the Committee and all who had testified against him in such "intemperate and provocative expressions" that Senator McCarran declared them to be Communist tactics. Lattimore termed Senator McCarthy "a graduate witch burner," attacked me as a perjurer, Stassen as irresponsible, and the Chinese Nationalists as "driftwood on the beaches of Formosa." He even extended his invective to people who had not appeared before the Committee, declaring that Senator William Knowland of California was known as "the Senator from Formosa," a favorite Communist sneer.

But when examination by Robert Morris, Committee counsel, showed numerous contradictions between Lattimore's testimony before the Tydings Committee in 1950 and documentary evidence from IPR files, the Johns Hopkins professor fell back on a "defective memory" as his defense. Although hailed officially and in his books as a Far Eastern expert and the man among living Americans who knew most about Asia, Lattimore asserted that he was "not an expert on Communism," the most vital question in Asia today.

A few of the many contradictions in Lattimore's testimony disclosed by Mr. Morris were the following:

1) Whereas he told the Tydings Committee he never had a desk in the State Department, as Senator McCarthy charged, now he conceded he had a desk in Lauchlin Currie's office, which was connected with that department, and answered mail from there.

2) Immediately after his appointment by President Roosevelt in 1941 as special representative to Chiang Kai-shek, Lattimore had a private conference with the Soviet Ambassador, Oumansky. Alleging that this was the result of "publicity" about his appointment, Mr. Morris promptly made him admit this could not be so, since there was no public reference to his appointment until eleven days after the Oumansky conference. Also contrary to Lattimore's previous sworn testimony, it was

shown that the meeting with the Soviet Ambassador took place on June 18, 1941, and therefore during the Hitler-Stalin Pact period, when Soviet Russia and the Communists were bitterly attacking the United States.

3) Lattimore also insisted that he discussed only the fact of his assignment and none of its details with the Soviet Ambassador. A written report by Edward C. Carter, who arranged the meeting, stated to Dr. Philip C. Jessup that the conference "was a most illuminating two hours."

4) Contrary to Lattimore's previous statements, it was also brought out that in a meeting held with Russian IPR officials in Moscow in 1936, Lattimore had asked them "if there was any interest in the USSR about questions of air bases in the Pacific." At the same conference, documentary evidence also showed that the Soviet geographer, V. E. Motylev, and the Comintern veteran, G. N. Voitinsky, insisted that there be "a more definite line" in the articles in *Pacific Affairs,* which Lattimore was then editing. To which Lattimore replied, according to the documentary evidence, that "if the Soviet group would start on such a line" he would be able "to co-operate more fully."

Then he was asked by Senator Homer Ferguson: "That line was the Communist Party line, wasn't it?" To which Lattimore replied: "In my opinion, no." Following other questions, he went so far as to assert: "The line of the Soviet council of the IPR . . . nothing Communist about it." And then, to cap it off, he stated: "I believe the Russians have at various times followed lines . . . that had nothing Communist about them."

These were amazing assertions, in view of the well-known complete control by Stalin and the Moscow Politburo of all Soviet thinking and Communist activities throughout the world.

5) In the executive session of the McCarran Subcommittee, Lattimore had sworn that he had made no "pre-arrangements" with the Chinese Communists for his 1937 trip to Red Yenan with Philip Jaffe and T. A. Bisson. This contradicted a letter he had written to the Communist authorities and which he had mentioned in an article in the *London Times* together with the Reds' "cordial invitation" to him to make the trip.

6) Lattimore denied that he had read the article by T. A. Bisson referring to Nationalist China as "feudal China" and Red China as "democratic China." In contradiction, Robert Morris produced a letter by Lattimore to W. L. Holland of the IPR stating that he had read Bisson's article, and seemingly expressing agreement with it.

7) Although the witness stated under oath that he did not know that the writer "Asiaticus" was the well-known Communist, Heinz Müller, a letter by Lattimore was produced which contradicted his assertion. It referred to an article by "a Communist" which was to appear in the specific issue of *Pacific Affairs* in which the Asiaticus contribution was published.

8) Mrs. Owen Lattimore had claimed that her husband had never met any Soviet Russians, and he had inserted this claim in his book, *Ordeal by Slander*. Examination brought out that this was strikingly false, Lattimore admitting that he had met with Soviet representatives on a number of occasions.

9) Although Communist infiltration of the IPR had been shown by evidence to have existed on a large scale, Lattimore contended that he did not know of any Communist in the organization as such. Even his close friend

and associate, Frederick Vanderbilt Field, was not recognized by him as a Communist, he claimed, until about 1941. Confronted with documentary evidence, he amended this statement by saying that he must have known Field's ideology as early as 1939. A few days later, Lattimore wanted to change the date back again. But *Time* magazine for March 10, 1952, gave a succinct account of the Field-Lattimore relationship when it said: "One IPR memo, from Field to Lattimore, read like an order: Discussing a certain article it cautioned Editor Lattimore that 'the analysis is a straight Marxist one and . . . should not be altered.' " It must be remembered that when Lattimore testified, four of his associates in the IPR had already refused to state to the committee under oath whether or not they were Communists, on the grounds it might "tend to incriminate them." These four were Lawrence K. Rosinger, former IPR research director and former UNRRA representative in China, a writer on the Far East; Kathleen Barnes, former wife of Joseph Barnes; Harriet Lucy Moore, active for a number of years as an executive of the IPR; and Frederick Vanderbilt Field, its secretary when Lattimore was editor of *Pacific Affairs*.

The McCarran Subcommittee, *Time* commented, through its examination of Lattimore, was "exposing what looked like a powerful Communist web of propaganda and persuasion" around the IPR and ultimately around U. S. policy making.

This congregation of Communists and pro-Communists in the IPR led to the naming of eighty persons by various witnesses before the McCarran Subcommittee, either as Communists or as so closely associated with the Communists as to be in the actively pro-Communist class. With such a corps of infiltrators in this organization, its activities went far beyond mere propaganda. For example, the IPR went all-out to obtain a commission for Frederick Vanderbilt Field in the Army Intelligence during World War II. At that time Fields' leadership in the American Peace Mobilization, Red-created front on behalf of Hitler, was known to all IPR officials and active members. His writings in the *New Masses* were also a matter of knowledge in informed circles. In spite of this, E. C. Carter, a directing officer of the IPR, Owen Lattimore, and William T. Stone, then in the State Department, worked for Field's appointment to this strategic position. Stone, incidentally, was associated with Lattimore, Jaffe, and Field on the board of *Amerasia*.

Field's hopes were dashed by a report of the Federal Bureau of Investigation disclosing his seditious connections. What he would have done against American security in an intelligence post can be gauged from the aid he gave as an officer of the IPR to Soviet espionage. The sworn statement of Alexander Barmine, ex-Red Army General, that the Russian military intelligence planned to use the IPR as a cover for its work in China is matched by revelations of events which took place here in which Field played a part.

This is brought out sharply in the testimony of Whittaker Chambers before the McCarran Subcommittee in regard to the recruiting of Laurence Duggan into Soviet espionage in the late thirties. Duggan held at that time a prominent position in the State Department. Chambers was working with the Soviet espionage apparatus in Washington, headed by the Russian, Colonel Boris Bykov of the Soviet Consulate. According to Chambers, the head of one unit of Bykov's espionage apparatus was Alger Hiss, who had made attempts to engage Duggan in his spy activities. The following transpired, as Chambers delineated it:

To repeat, Colonel Bykov decided to make another attempt to recruit Laurence Duggan for his apparatus. In persuance of that effort, I talked to J. Peters. J. Peters was the head of the underground section of the American Communist Party. Peters knew that Fred Vanderbilt Field and Laurence Duggan were friends and told me so.

It may be interjected here that they were friends through their relationship with each other in the Institute of Pacific Relations in which correspondence shows Duggan was interested.

Chambers continued:

I then asked Peters to introduce me to Frederick Vanderbilt Field, and that Peters did in New York City close to Park Avenue and 34th Street. I then had lunch with Fred Vanderbilt Field, but before I go into our conversation at lunch, perhaps I should go a little further into what Peters told me about Field in the course of a general, casual conversation in discussing Frederick Vanderbilt Field. Peters told me that Field was a member of an underground unit of the American Communist Party, which was meeting, if I remember correctly, in a house belonging to Mr. Field's mother somewhere in Central Park West, New York. In that unit were Frederick Vanderbilt Field and Joseph Barnes.

This is what happened:

I had, as I said, lunch with Frederick Vanderbilt Field, and asked him to go to Washington and try to recruit for the Bykov apparatus Laurence Duggan in the State Department. Field, as nearly as I can remember now, left either that day or the next day for Washington, and I saw him a day or two later. He told me that he had had a long conversation with Laurence Duggan, and that Laurence Duggan said that he could do nothing for the Bykov apparatus because he was already connected with another apparatus.

It turned out that this was the Soviet spy ring for which Hede Massing, the former wife of Gerhart Eisler, was recruiting at that time, 1937. Mrs. Massing confirmed this testimony under oath, as she had done previously in her book. It was over the question of what group Duggan should co-operate with that she had the quarrel with Alger Hiss.

Other testimony indicates that Frederick Vanderbilt Field was engaged in still further espionage work with J. Peters, discussing couriers to Washington with him and with Philip Jaffe.

The whole episode involving Duggan and the events connected with it are most pertinent to an estimate of the Institute of Pacific Relations as a channel through which the Communists worked. They reveal not only that an active member of the IPR, working in the State Department, was by authoritative accusation guilty of espionage; but also that the secretary of the IPR, Frederick Vanderbilt Field, was engaged in such activity.

Among active members of the Institute of Pacific Relations, several were found to be members of the notorious Richard Sorge spy ring, with its center in Japan but with outlets on the Asiatic continent. As a matter of fact, China was the ring's recruiting ground. The late Agnes Smedley, reputedly a newspaper correspondent, actually a veteran in Soviet espionage, was its chief recruiter. Miss Smedley was an active member of the IPR and much valued in its councils.

The story of this amazing and successful adventure in Soviet espionage is now available in sworn testimony by Major General Charles Willoughby, Chief of Intelligence for the Far East Command under General Douglas MacArthur, who unearthed spy data, and by Mitsuda Yoshikawa, director of the Special Investigation Bureau of the Japanese Attorney General's Office. Yoshikawa assisted in the unearthing of the Sorge ring in Japan, which led to statements by Sorge explaining the ring and to his execution. In brief, the story runs as follows:

Richard Sorge was a secret German Communist, well known in Red underground circles and assigned by the Soviet Government to the Far East. He was directly connected with the Intelligence Section of the Soviet Army with the rank of Colonel. By getting himself named as press attaché of the German Embassy in Tokyo he gained entree into official Japanese circles. Through Agnes Smedley, he was introduced to Hotsumi Ozaki, who became his right-hand man. Miss Smedley was also instrumental in securing the services for his ring of one Teikishi Kawai, who is still living and whose affidavit aided the American authorities in their investigation. The events described took place in 1941, but the investigation occurred after the American occupation of Japan.

Proceeding with the story: Ozaki, Sorge's right-hand man, was an old college friend of two prominent members of the Japanese IPR who had been recommended by E. C. Carter to the international secretariat of the Institute. These were Ushiba and Saionji, influential in the Japanese Cabinet. Thus Sorge was in a position to obtain valuable information from many sources in Tokyo and even to assist in the course of events.

Soviet Russia was most eager that Japan should attack the United States through the Philippines rather than the Soviet Union by way of Siberia. On the various possibilities Sorge kept a careful check, and by October 15, 1941, he was able to advise the Soviet government that Japan had decided to move south and attack the United States. He transmitted this information to Moscow, according to his usual custom, through radio messages sent by Max Klausen, whose disappearance from Japan via the Soviet Embassy led to General Willoughby's investigations. At least thirty of these messages were sent to the Soviet capital from the home of Gunther Stein, British newspaper correspondent and prominent in the American IPR. For a time Stein was the official correspondent of the IPR in the Far East and contributed twenty-one articles over ten years to the official publications of that organization. Through IPR sources his writings on the Far East favorable to the Communists were distributed through the Office of War Information at the very time when he was engaging in his activities as a member of the Sorge ring.

Soviet Russia thus had information on the Pearl Harbor attack *two months before* it occurred, but "our gallant ally" did not transmit the information to the United States government. Valuable data that would have been enormously helpful to our armed forces, such as the shortage of petroleum in the Japanese navy, was likewise withheld from us by Soviet Russia.

Three days after the final accomplishment of his two-year mission Sorge was arrested as a spy, interrogated, and in 1944 executed. Through his interrogation and that of some of his associates the Japanese authorities were able to learn of the extent and character of his work. This was later supplemented by what General Willoughby's investigation disclosed.

While Soviet Russia was so deeply interested in seeing that Japan "moved south" to attack the United States, high officials and prominent members of the IPR were eagerly seeking to prevent the United States from accepting a proposed ninety-day truce with Japan. On November 25, 1941, Owen Lattimore cabled his friend, Lauchlin Currie, then executive assistant to the President, urging that the truce proposal be rejected. Harry Dexter White, then Under Secretary of the Treasury, summoned E. C. Carter to Washington and asked him to use his influence and efforts to prevent any "sell-out of China." That could only mean that Japan would be put in the position of feeling it necessary to attack the United States. Each of these three—Lattimore, who was then personal adviser to Chiang Kai-shek through American suggestion, Currie, then executive assistant to the President, and White—has been identified as connected with the Communist cell in the IPR or with the Communist underground apparatus.

Sorge's work in Japan in this way dovetailed with the frantic efforts of these prominent IPR people to bring on Pearl Harbor.

It is quite evident that the Communists and their friends used the IPR as a base to advance the cause of the Chinese Communists. This activity and others that went with it caused Jacob Golos, chairman of the Control Commission of the Communist Party, to warn Elizabeth Bentley that the Institute could not be used extensively for obtaining espionage agents, since it had become "red as a rose." The part that the organization played on behalf of the Reds in China was naïvely admitted by E. C. Carter when he agreed that Lattimore's letter commending him for following the Chinese Communist views was "a bouquet" handed him for following the Communist line on China.

A helping agent was Michael Greenberg, Communist alien, who became editor of *Pacific Affairs* and then the successor to Frederick Vanderbilt Field as executive secretary of the American section of the IPR. From there he moved into the Board of Economic Warfare and later (having become a citizen) was appointed to a position in the White House itself, in the office of Lauchlin Currie.

In the period of Lattimore's editorship, the IPR publications and pamphlets often lent themselves to articles directly or indirectly criticizing the Chiang Kai-shek regime or representing the Chinese Communists as not connected with Moscow. One of these contributions in the official publication of the IPR, *Pacific Affairs,* drew protests from China's representatives in this country. This was a very important article for its time, published in the July 14, 1943 issue of *Far Eastern Survey,* an official journal of the American Council of the Institute of Pacific Relations. Its author was T. A. Bisson, who had accompanied Owen Lattimore and Philip Jaffe on the trip to Yenan which had given such encouragement to the Chinese Communists in 1937. In this article, Bisson declared categorically that Nationalist China was "feudal China," and Red China "democratic China." This was precisely the Communist terminology used subsequently by Lattimore through a study conducted at Johns Hopkins University.

A good example of the manner in which the Communists penetrated the government is furnished by the case of Mildred Price. She was in an executive position in the IPR and at the same time openly associated with the China Aid Council, a Communist-created group which made few bones about its trends or purposes. In the Communist cell in the IPR Miss Price was second in command to Frederick Vanderbilt Field. According to testimony of Elizabeth Bentley, confirmed by other witnesses, directives to the IPR were issued personally by Earl Browder through Frederick Vanderbilt Field to Miss Price, although Field at that time held no position in the IPR. But this work went further, and Miss Price took on the role of courier for the Soviet underground, relaying information obtained from Michael Greenberg (in Lauchlin Currie's office) at the White House to Elizabeth Bentley for the benefit of the Soviet Consulate. The data furnished by Greenberg in this specific instance had to do with Far Eastern affairs.

Mildred Price was also active in obtaining from Red China information of a confidential character which the Chinese Nationalists would not permit to leave that country. According to Miss Bentley's testimony, this information, largely obtained from Madame Sun Yat-sen, whose work for the Communists is well known, was delivered by John K. Fairbank, an active participant in the IPR. Fairbank was then head of the China division of the Office of War Information.

Not the least of those in public posts who built himself up through membership on the board of directors of the IPR was Alger Hiss. Official correspondence and records disclose Hiss as an adviser to the Institute in its policies and programs, particularly in arranging its series of public conferences. His aid was even solicited to safeguard the status of an alien with a clouded record, whom Carter wanted to address that conference. Hiss' intervention, as a State Department official, was sought since it was feared that this alien might be deported from Canada. Carter was also very eager to have Hiss confer with Vladimir Rogoff, Soviet agent in charge of Far Eastern affairs in the United States, and at that time correspondent for Tass, the Russian official news agency.

Still another man in government who ran errands for the Communists was O. Edmund Clubb of the State Department. When Whittaker Chambers swore that Clubb had brought information, presumably from Agnes Smedley, when he was in the Soviet underground and on the staff of the *New Masses,* Clubb first denied the accusation. But a subsequent look at his diaries compelled him to change his testimony and to acknowledge that he had served as a courier for Miss Smedley.

As an official of the IPR, Carter quite frankly admitted, and correspondence bore out his admission, that he had consulted Chinese Communists as to policy before submitting suggestions to American officials, notably Lauchlin Currie. A network of communications, which could not but influence the State Department or various sections thereof, was revealed extending from Moscow and the Red leaders here, through the IPR, into government offices. For instance, of those who worked closest with Mildred Price and Frederick Vanderbilt Field was Harriet Lucy Moore, identified as a Communist, and serving on the executive committee of the Institute as well as on its nominating committee for several years. She was sent to Moscow by the IPR, even though her open pro-Soviet sympathies were disclosed in articles written for *Soviet Russia Today,* a Communist-controlled magazine similar to those set up by Moscow throughout the world.

Symbolic of how IPR people wove themselves into the official American fabric are the operations of Owen Lattimore and John K. Fairbank from Lauchlin Currie's offices in the White House. They were placed in Currie's office, receiving their mail and sending communications from that address. Another IPR staff member, Lawrence K. Rosinger, research director there for some time, first changed places with T. A. Bisson at the Foreign Policy Association and then became a representative of the United Nations Relief Authority (UNRRA) in China. Before the McCarran Subcommittee on January 28, 1952, Rosinger refused to answer whether he was or was not a member of the Communist Party. He joined the long list of those who declared that an answer would tend to incriminate them.

During the time that Field was executive secretary of the IPR and Greenberg served as his successor, Dr. Philip Jessup, American Ambassador at Large, was chairman of that body. The charges made by Harold E. Stassen, former Governor of Minnesota, on top of other allegations against Jessup, caused his rejection by a vote of three to two by the Senate Subcommittee hearing his case. It is significant that the Democratic Senator from Iowa, Guy M. Gillette, who is noted for his independent judgment, cast the deciding vote. Leaving aside the question of whether or not Jessup was inveigled into joining certain Communist fronts without fully knowing their character, as he contends, the record shows his close and sympathetic association with Field and those thinking like him in the IPR. This went to the extent of Dr. Jessup's acquiescing in the declaration that Field had gone to engage in "democratic activities" when he became the directing head of the obviously Communist-created American Peace Mobilization in 1940. Considering this attitude and Dr. Jessup's desire that Field return to the IPR when his work on behalf of the Hitler-Stalin Pact was finished, it is not illogical that Jessup should have prepared the White Paper, which so severely castigated the Chinese Nationalists and in effect was an apology for the abandonment of China to the Communists.

The interest of large industrialists, Wall Street lawyers, and presidents of universities in the IPR has been cited as proof that it could not have been penetrated successfully by the Communists. This is a grave misjudgment of Communist astuteness. The very naming of these public-spirited men was an immeasurable asset to the Communists infiltrating the working machine of the Institute. It made much more impressive the propaganda that emanated from the IPR in favor of Red China under the guise of "free inquiry." It made much easier the task of making the IPR a cover for underground contacts. Industrialists, Wall Street lawyers, and presidents of universities are busy with their own pursuits. They cannot, and do not, give to the work of an organization that full-time energy which the Reds devote to any group they mean to influence or control. It is notorious that most of the men who have leading posts in industry, corporation law, and education are tragically uninformed on the techniques of the Communists and of the Communist line at any particular period. This can permit concealed Reds, or even those so openly Communist as Frederick Vanderbilt Field, to commit organizations with which these leading citizens are conected to pro-Communist purposes.

From the record, that is clearly what happened in the case of the Institute of Pacific Relations.

# CHAPTER 4

# *Our Law Helps the Reds*

Judith Coplon, Soviet espionage agent, is a symbol of the ability of the Red fifth column to defeat American security provisions. With the usual ease of infiltration, Miss Coplon had obtained by the spring of 1949 a position in the Department of Justice where she had ready access to confidential files.

In 1949 she came to New York one day, as she had been doing for some time, to meet Valentin A. Gubitchev, a Russian Communist who had got into the United States with a Soviet delegation to the United Nations, and then been transferred to its technical staff as an engineer. On this last meeting, Gubitchev and Miss Coplon were finally apprehended by agents of the Federal Bureau of Investigation. They were arrested on the street as Miss Coplon was preparing to pass to Gubitchev documents from the confidential files of the Department of Justice.

Although protracted trials led to conviction of Miss Coplon for espionage activities, and although the judges who passed upon her appeal agreed with the juries that she was guilty, she is today a free citizen. The United States Supreme Court held that the FBI agent should have had a warrant when he took this spy into custody.

An ordinary citizen has the legal right at all times to arrest anyone whom he sees committing a crime, or whom he observes engaged in a criminal act. The men from the Federal Bureau of Investigation are not permitted to do this; they must first get a warrant. This often consumes valuable time. And since there was one Judith Coplon in the Department of Justice, there may be more—and some of them may be in the offices of magistrates who issue warrants. If the FBI is compelled to apply for this document in espionage cases, the possibility of catching spies is very much limited.

To remedy this defect Congress passed new legislation to aid the FBI. Whether this will prove to be fully effective remains to be seen.

The Coplon case underscores one weakness in our security laws as interpreted by the courts. That weakness is further exemplified by the defiant refusal of those accused of espionage to testify against their fellow conspirators. In this, too, they have been upheld by the law, and cases against them have consequently collapsed. As it stands today, by using a little skill in their operations Soviet agents from abroad and their contacts in this country may function freely.

Another factor in the Coplon case illustrates the low level of security precautions in Washington. Only a few months before Miss Coplon's arrest, she had been highly commended by her immediate superiors to Barnard College, her alma mater. They had emphasized her judgment and reliability.

What the Coplon decision has done to aid Soviet espionage, the ruling in the case of William W. Remington has done to favor Red infiltration in the government. Remington first came to national attention four years ago when Elizabeth Bentley, in the course of her revelations on espionage in Washington, mentioned him as one of her contacts. Remington, who held a $10,000-a-year job in a rather sensitive post in the Department of Commerce, engaged in passing on the shipping of goods to Russia, was suspended. The President's Loyalty Board, then under the chairmanship of Seth Richardson, promptly cleared him and he was reinstated. Shortly thereafter, information came into the possession of the House Committee on Un-American Activities and the Department of Justice that a number of individuals in various phases of Remington's career had known him as a Communist. This included associates at Dartmouth College, when he was employed by the Tennessee Valley Authority, and in the national capital. A chief witness against him was his former wife, Anna Moos Remington, whose mother is an active Red. Mrs. Remington had also been infatuated with Communist doctrines but had broken away. Being presented with such overwhelming evidence by eyewitnesses from so many parts of the country, the jury convicted Remington of perjury for having sworn that he was not and never had been a Communist.

The Federal Circuit Court of Appeals, however, promptly set aside the verdict. In criticizing the charge of the trial judge to the jury, the court said in effect that a much clearer showing of party membership was required. Although the decision is vague, it seems to make necessary a complicated and difficult method of proof, in order to show that one is a party member. If that is the case, the concealed Communists will have a Roman holiday, since most of the members of the conspiracy have well disguised visible signs of membership, and today the Communist Party security regulations have practically abolished them. Remington was not reinstated in his Department of Commerce post, being removed on a technicality. It is certain he will be tried again. But it requires no argument to show that such a state of affairs in the legal system handicaps the discovery of concealed Communists who are this country's greatest menace today.

The concealed Reds in the labor movement are also in a peculiarly privileged position, as far as legal action goes. In 1951 leaders of all the unions which had been expelled from the CIO for Red control announced that they had resigned from the Communist Party. Even Ben Gold, president of the Fur and Leather Workers Union, and Donald Henderson, secretary-treasurer of the Distributive Workers Union, made such declarations. The purpose was obvious; it was to defeat the non-Communist oath provisions of the Taft-Hartley Act. Each one of these men, after his alleged resignation, filed the non-Communist oath and the National Labor Relations Board accepted the affidavits on their face value. As a consequence, Communists have been left in control of wide areas of the labor movement, where they are able to paralyze key industries when Stalin's needs require it.

The *Daily Worker* quite blandly explained why the resignation had been carried through. That they were highly approved of by the leaders of the party was indicated by the big play each resignation got in the pages of their newspaper. Some Communists of the rank-and-file, particularly in the Furniture Workers Union, became confused by the maneuver, and apparently felt that they too were to conceal their Red affiliations from their fellow workers. The *Daily Worker* disabused them of this idea. They were told that the leaders had to deny the party publicly for the protection of the whole group, but the ordinary member was to continue even more vigorously to carry on the work. Needless to say, of course, such work shall be conducted discreetly, so that the security regulations of the conspiracy may not be violated.

The dishonest character of these resignations is quite evident when one remembers the Communist practice of denouncing as "renegades," "traitors," and "opportunists," any persons who genuinely withdrew from the conspiracy. Genuine ex-Communists are hounded with a character assassination campaign of gangster proportions. But Gold, Henderson, Max Perlow of the Furniture Workers Union, and Julius Emspak and James Matles of the UE are still praised publicly by the conspiracy. Their work is applauded. And the National Labor Relations Board refuses to look behind their oaths, to determine their validity.

This trick used to protect Red leaders in the labor movement is also employed on behalf of people like Coplon and Remington. People may be secret members of the party, or they may be non-members by secret agreement with the party. Our law takes no cognizance of this reality. Thus the United States is legally handicapped in curbing the Reds in some of the most important fields of their subversive activity.

When it comes to deporting illegal aliens, who are directing Stalin's conspiracy in this country, the legal snarl is just as bad. The peculiar impotence of the United States in this matter is revealed in an article in the September, 1951, issue of *Political Affairs*, official theoretical organ of the Communist Party. The article is by Alexander Bittelman, chief theoretician for the Communists in this country. Bittelman gives directives to the Communists to intensify their activities against the United States, suggesting that this can best be carried out in the coming elections through a "people's peace coalition." He means that the Progressive Party, which is completely controlled by the Communists, shall be used to bring about wider political alliances favorable to them and to Soviet Russia. Bittelman himself cannot even vote in the election about which he writes so glibly. He is an illegal alien, a Soviet citizen who has been living in this country for many years because of the inability of the United States to get rid of him. He was, indeed, tried for deportation and ordered deported. But he has, of course, appealed to the United States Supreme Court, and meanwhile, everyone knows that he *cannot* be deported, since Soviet Russia will refuse to receive him. The Kremlin will take this position because it wants him here.

Bittelman has done immeasurable damage to the United States while remaining at large. In November, 1950, for instance, he called for a "peace crusade" to off-set "Wall Street's war crusade and aggression in Korea." Despite the fantastic character of the charge that the United States was the aggressor in the Korean war, his call was heeded. By January, 1951, the American Peace Crusade had been launched, and many educators, scientists, and other public figures were participating. Among them were Robert Morss Lovett, former government secretary of the Virgin Islands, and Dr. Philip Morrison of Cornell University. The crusade organized a pilgrimage to Washington to demand withdrawal of American troops from Korea and recognition of Red China. The pilgrimage also approached congressmen and senators urging against the extension of the draft, the sending of American troops to Europe, and the rearmament of West Germany. Such demands were exact echoes of what Moscow had been flashing through the world in the pages of the Cominform's directive organ. They were the fulfillment of Bittelman's orders, and they worked in with countless other "peace" organizations created by Bittelman and his

Red associates. Thus the inability of the United States to deport Bittelman has been a major aid to the Communist conspiracy in its work of creating illusions, uncertainties, and paralysis of action among the American people.

This chief theoretician of the Communist Party is one of one hundred and fifty subversive aliens who have recently been ordered deported, but are free in this country today. The Department of Justice reported in 1950 that more than one thousand subversive aliens had been ordered deported, were under deportation proceedings, or were being looked into for deportation—all without much hope that any would leave the United States.

The record shows that of the very few Red aliens who have actually left this country, practically all left under orders from the Communist international apparatus. It was Soviet Russia which beckoned them back, not the United States which put them out. Take for a first example, Gerhart Eisler, Comintern representative in this country; his departure was in defiance of the government. He was under conviction for two offenses, but the bail was set so low that it invited his escape. When Eisler fled on the Polish ship, *Batory,* one of the most alert and able enemies of the United States was free to function against us in Central Europe.

J. Peters was a colleague of Eisler's in the American Comintern machine, directing its espionage work. He operated here for years without molestation, and when his deportation hearing was finally held, his attorney, the late Carol Weiss King, intimated that he would carry the case to the Supreme Court. That would cause at least two more years' delay. Moreover he was slated for deportation to Red Hungary, which could have carried out the usual maneuver of refusing to admit him. But Stalin needed him in Central Europe, and so he too went back voluntarily.

It was the same with John Santo, Rumanian-born alien, another important member of the Comintern set-up here, and Ferucci Marini, Italian-born alien, who directed the American organizational work for Moscow. The same with Boleslav Gebert, whom the United States tried in vain to deport in the thirties but who went on the *Batory* when the Kremlin called, his new job being to direct the planning for the disruption of the American economy.

Each of these men defied American orders for deportation, and in leaving proved that it is Stalin, and not our government, that controls the traveling of illegal aliens to and from the United States. A classical example of American impotence in this matter is the case of A. W. Mills, whose real name is Saul Milgrim. Because of his extensive subversive activities, including expert direction of violent demonstrations and instigation of strikes against our defense economy during the Hitler-Stalin Pact period, Mills was ordered for deportation as early as 1936. But the country to which he was to be sent, Soviet Russia, refused to accept him, as was to be expected. Mills was then permitted to extend his subversive activities, becoming national secretary of the International Workers Order, which has been ruled an adjunct of the Communist Party by New York Supreme Court Judge Henry Clay Greenberg. Ferdinand C. Smith, Claudia Jones, Betty Gannett, and scores of other leading Communist functionaries of alien status have similarly remained in this country in spite of deportation proceedings.

There is a remedy at hand for this grave situation which has really become highly critical with the many Soviet and satellite consulates and embassies opened here.

It is to be found in the Hobbs Bill, which has lingered in Congress for a dozen years. This bill would give the Attorney General power to jail aliens who are ordered for deportation, but are refused admission by their native countries. It would also forbid courts to grant bail to aliens after a deportation order, pending appeal. With the Hobbs Bill in effect, Gerhart Eisler could not have escaped. Thus it is not because the United States is without legislative recourse that we find ourselves in this predicament. It is because the American nation has not yet decided to defend itself against the greatest of its dangers, the enemy within its borders.

These Red aliens are the real rulers of the Communist conspiracy. It is they who create political strikes to paralyze our industry: it is they who will direct the sabotage against our defenses. We are completely unprepared, despite our alert Federal Bureau of Investigation, to cope with the organized panic, defeatism, and sabotage, which they would set going, should frontal war break out with the Soviet dictatorship.

Unfortunately President Truman, in his message of August 8, 1950, specifically insisted on the defeat of the Hobb's Bill. He held that it was "repugnant to our traditions," but that statement can scarcely stand scrutiny. Never has the American republic failed to find a means within its Constitution and traditions to defend itself from enemies in wartime. And since World War III is now on, fought by the Kremlin with weapons that undermine nations internally, the Hobbs Bill is entirely in line with our traditions. It is not nearly so drastic as President Lincoln's suspension of the writ of habeas corpus, in order to curb the Copperheads in the Civil War. These Red aliens are the experts in Stalin's campaign of sabotage. They are sent here to instruct the American

Communists in the art of destroying this republic. No clearer or more present danger exists.

In all these victories, the Communists have made much use of their favorite weapon—delay. The Communist considers our courts and government agencies a part of the state machinery which must be "smashed," as Lenin and Stalin have explicitly stated. He enters the courtroom determined to frustrate this machinery and make a mockery of the proceedings. He regards this as practice in the tactics he will use when the seizure of power is at hand. Meanwhile he delays his defeat and wins time to create confusion and division. These are the methods employed by the Reds in *internal psychological warfare*.

The classic example of Red delay tactics was the trial in Foley Square which lasted most of the year 1949. That trial opened in January, and for two months Communist counsel consumed the time of the court in endless wrangling, accusations, and loudly shouted arguments about our method of selecting a jury. This was one of the most astounding scenes ever witnessed in an American courtroom. The argument of the Communists was that the jury panels had been drawn up so as to exclude workers, the unemployed, Negroes, and women. The absurdity of their contention was revealed when the jury was finally chosen. The forewoman of the jury was a Negro woman, and there were workers, unemployed persons, and other women among the members. After protracted delay on this question of the jury, the trial finally got under way on March 23. Then the obstruction began all over again.

Nothing exemplifies better the mob scenes staged by defense counsel and by the defendants before Judge Harold Medina than the following colloquy during the examination of the first government witness. The Federal District Attorney, John F. X. McGohey, was asking the witness whether, when he mentioned the "ninth floor of the *Daily Worker*," he meant the "ninth floor of the building housing the national Communist Party." Before Mr. McGohey could complete this question, he was interrupted by Harry Sacher, the most violent of the Communist lawyers, and this is what ensued:

MR. SACHER: Your Honor, this man, Mr. Gordon, Assistant Federal District Attorney, just turned around and pointed his finger at me and said: "Sit down." I want to call that to the Court's attention. I will not permit myself to be terrorized by counsel for the Government.

THE COURT: I see you are returning to your old role.

MR. SACHER: I object to your Honor's remark and I ask your Honor to instruct the jury to disregard your statement.

THE COURT: Mr. Sacher, I dislike shouting and disorder and I will not tolerate it. I don't know what little passage may have occurred between counsel here, but there is no conceivable justification for your carrying on this way.

MR. SACHER: Your Honor, Mr. Gordon turned around and he faced me and waved his finger at me and said "Sit down."

MR. GORDON: That is not so.

DEFENDANT GATES: You're a liar.

THE COURT: You have waved your finger at me and that doesn't bother me. I don't see why you get so excited.

MR. SACHER: Well, your Honor—

THE COURT: Let's let these little incidents evaporate and not occur any more.

MR. SACHER: May I respectfully ask that you tell the Government to desist from facing defendants' counsel. Their back is supposed to be turned to me and I prefer to see that part of them.

THE COURT: You see how one thing may lead to another without profit to anyone. We get into a dispute as to whether something was said or whether it was not. I think the wiser course to pursue is let's forget it.

MR. McGOHEY: I was going to ask the Court to direct that

counsel refrain from characterizing the witness. It was a characterization that I asked the Court to strike out.

THE COURT: Fortunately I didn't hear it and whatever it was is directed to be stricken out. If anyone of the jurors heard anything they will put it from their mind.[1]

Such outbursts, accompanied by fist-shaking and loud accusations of unfairness occurred at each session. Several of the defendants were found guilty of contempt and their bail was suspended for several days, but that did not halt the torrent of abuse they hurled at both witnesses and court. Four of the five defense lawyers were subsequently sentenced for contempt and their appeals rejected by the Supreme Court. Disbarment proceedings were also begun against them, but it was only in April, 1952, that they began to serve their sentences.

Many commentators and observers suggested that this rowdyism was injurious to the Communists in public opinion, and that the Reds had been unwise to employ such tactics. They do not understand the Red objectives, the more immediate of which are to cause confusion and delay. The convictions were not obtained until mid-October of 1949. Subsequent appeals postponed the final jailing of the convicted men for two years. This was precious time gained for the party. During that period it was able to build up its reserves, and train its substitutes for these men when they should go off to serve their sentences. Since the conspiracy is built on military lines, this system of reserve cadres is a vital feature of its operation. In the big purge trials of the so-called Trotskyists and Bukharinites in Moscow in 1937 and 1938, the Soviet government charged the accused with having formed concentric rings, the secondary and tertiary of which were to take the place of the first and second in case of ex-

[1] This colloquy is reprinted from the record of the trial.

posure. That is precisely the manner in which the Stalin-
ite apparatus is organized in America and in every other
non-Soviet country. Judge Medina's patience and self-
control were morally admirable, but the time gained
suited the purposes of the Communists, to practice up for
the "smashing of the bourgeois state."

During the Hitler-Stalin Pact, when the Communist
organization set plans to "turn the imperialist war into
civil war" within the United States, this method of reserves was intensively developed. Testimony shows that
the American Peace Mobilization, whose secretary was
then Frederick Vanderbilt Field, was to serve as a legal
cover to hold these reserves together when they should
have to function underground. Another Red adjunct,
the International Workers Order, was also to serve in
this capacity.

At the beginning of the present period, which is regarded as that of World War III, this reserve system was
promptly put into effect. Esther Cantor, who had been a
writer on the *Daily Worker* staff in the forties, and then
a section organizer of the party, came forward in June,
1951, in a new and larger role. She replaced some of
those who before their arrest had been directing Communist propaganda among Negroes in New York City and
thence throughout the nation. Sid Stein, only a few years
ago an obscure section organizer in New Jersey, emerged
as Communist labor commissar, at least temporarily, in
the place of John Williamson, one of the jailed eleven.
Out in the Illinois district, considered of prime importance in controlling the Midwest centers of basic production, Claude Lightfoot took the place of Gil Green, one
of the four convicted Reds who jumped bail. Lightfoot
had long been chairman of the Young Communist League
in Illinois, and was subsequently advanced to other posts

in that district. He had been a student at the Lenin School in Moscow, and had taken special courses in the strategy of violence in the secret training school of the Illinois district. This last training took place in 1938, which shows how long Lightfoot was in the process of preparation for the post of Red leader in the district.

The value of delay comes up again in the case of Harold Christoffel. Expelled from the Socialist Party because he was a Communist, Christoffel became during the Hitler-Stalin Pact a leading figure on behalf of Hitler in halting American production. As president of the local union of the United Automobile Workers at the Allis-Chalmers plant in Milwaukee, he shut down all production in 1941 by a fraudulently-voted strike. Six years later, he appeared before the House Committee on Labor and Education and swore that he was not and never had been a member of the Communist Party. But evidence brought out at the same hearing disclosed that he was a Communist, and had conferred secretly with Eugene Dennis, representing the Politburo, on arrangements for the strike. It was on Dennis' orders that he had started the strike. As a consequence, he was indicted for perjury.

At his trial in 1948, a number of witnesses identified him as a Communist, and he put up no real defense. He was speedily convicted in a Washington, D.C. federal court, but the Supreme Court of the United States came to his rescue. By the unsatisfactory vote of five to four, our highest tribunal supported Justice Frank Murphy's contention that the question whether there had been a quorum of the committee present when Christoffel committed his perjury should not have been decided by the trial judge but left to the jury. On that minute point, so obscure legally as to bring about the close division in the court, Christoffel was remanded for a new trial.

This type of strained legalism, of which the Communists have frequently been the beneficiaries, is represented as a "defense of civil liberties." The Reds take advantage of it to declare that they have been "vindicated" by the courts. This happened in the case of Christoffel. On the basis of his alleged vindication, thousands of dollars were collected in the legitimate labor movement and elsewhere for his defense as "a labor martyr." In addition, he was appointed by the Politburo to the post of secretary of the committee of the Communist-created Civil Rights Congress, which defended the eleven Communist leaders. He became, that is, an important member of the reserve. With their usual arrogance, the leaders of the party gave him this obviously pro-Communist function even while he was contending that he was not a Communist.

In 1949, a new trial took place, and Christoffel was convicted even more speedily than before, and by a jury composed of the very types of people whom the Communists contend are never put on such juries. But again the law's delays and technicalities intervened, and Christoffel, though under indictment for perjury, is still at large. His attorney, O. John Rogge, went off to the Communist peace congress in Stockholm, returned pro-Tito, and did not appear when Christoffel's appeal came up. The Communists could easily have obtained another lawyer, but they saw a chance for further procrastination. No one showed up to press Christoffel's appeal, and his case was temporarily thrown out of court. After a considerable further delay, a new lawyer turned up in the Court of Appeals, and asked that the case be reinstated on the calendar. The appeal court agreed, gently reprimanding Rogge for negligence. Thus more time had been gained, during which Christoffel could serve the Communist conspiracy.

This loose attitude of certain courts in Communist cases has greatly strengthened the conspiracy during the last several years. By the middle of 1950, the Communists had reached their lowest ebb in the labor movement, but in 1951 they made gains for their Red-ruled unions. Most striking was what took place at the General Electric Company in Schenectady, where circumstances have compelled the corporation to take a neutral attitude toward the United Electrical, Radio, and Machine Workers of America. That organization, expelled from the CIO because of Communist control, was victorious in the National Labor Relations Board election, defeating the CIO union 11,000 to 4,000. This occurred even though one of the leaders of that union, Ruth Young, had been publicly reported by the Reds as chairman of one of their State Convention meetings. Her pro-Communist record is well known. The other local leader, her husband, Leo Jandreau, has been identified in sworn testimony as a member of the Communist Party. The national officers of the UE had, on more than one occasion, refused to tell congressional committees whether or not they were Communists, and been charged with contempt. But the courts had let them off on technicalities, and this was widely represented by the Reds as a vindication. It was so represented in Schenectady through the *Daily Worker,* and furnished an argument in the election.

It is under this banner of "vindication" that the Communists are making a marked comeback in their activities in the labor movement. Even in the case of the eleven convicted leaders, the long wait for a final decision in the Supreme Court was made use of for Communist agitation. The Mine, Mill, and Smelter Workers Union, expelled from the CIO, took the lead in declaring that the conviction of the eleven had been a blow to all labor. Communists and friends of Communists in other unions, still affiliated with the CIO and AFL, made the same declarations. The officers of the big Ford Local 600 at River Rouge, with its 80,000 members, were among those conspicuously joining in these declarations. In that huge local, the Reds have extended their influence and its secretary, William Hood,[2] became prominent in many pro-Communist moves, including a leading position on the Negro Labor Committee, Red-created. Another labor official who denounced the jailing of the eleven Communists is none other than President Hugo Ernst of the Hotel and Restaurant Employees of the AFL, who made his declaration editorially in the August issue of that union's official journal.

Thus the prolonged defense of the eleven was turned into a defense of all Reds, including those penetrating particular unions. The same thing occurred in non-labor organizations.

This campaign of agitation and propaganda was promoted by the happy fate of Communists who defied Congress. In the 1950 report of the House Committee on Un-American Activities, it is stated that during that one year fifty-eight persons had been cited for contempt of Congress for refusing to declare under oath whether or not they were Communists. All of them had also refused to answer other pertinent questions. Of this number only a few were convicted; the rest were freed by the courts. The ground on which they were freed was an

---

2 In March, 1952, as a result of a Detroit investigation by the House Committee on Un-American Activities, the national office of the United Auto Workers placed Local 600 under an administrator. This was a move to end Red control there.

acceptance of their plea that any answers they might give would "tend to incriminate them." This plea has run like a chant through the hearings of congressional committees, notably the House Committee on Un-American Activities. It has been made by actors, writers, scientists accused of espionage, by the former secretary of the Institute of Pacific Relations, and by Communist Party functionaries in "mass organizations." Through this device, the Communists and their allies have succeeded in suppressing the full story of their widespread infiltration and espionage. A series of refusals to answer, even though the questions themselves when unanswered are most enlightening, is not good news copy. As a consequence, the press gives small attention to what the committees are seeking to expose. The American people are thus kept largely in the dark as to the character and extent of Communist influence and infiltration.

The attitude of the courts in these matters is merely one more aspect of the general American weakness of not understanding the Communist conspiracy. The various decisions of the Supreme Court on the question of self-incrimination are confusing and conflicting, and the question is really left to the discretion of the trial judge and his opinion of the "good faith" of the person making the plea. An understanding of the nature of the conspiracy would change completely the courts' present attitude in regard to this "good faith."

It is quite obvious that our law, in its practical application, has not taken into consideration the basic reality. This was made clear by the Supreme Court decision upholding the Smith Act and the conviction of the eleven Communist leaders under it. That decision says in effect that the Communist Party is a criminal conspiracy against the security of the United States and a clear and present danger to the nation. Few of the Communist cases are treated in this light; they are treated as individual offenses and not the acts of conspirators.

This weakness in our legal processes is increased by the lengthy and repetitious methods prescribed for conducting Red trials. Even though the criminally conspiratorial character of the Communist organization is now established, it remains necessary in each subsequent case to repeat the testimony to that effect. In the hearings before the Subversive Activities Control Board, it is considered essential to go through the whole process of proving all over again the conspiratorial character of the Soviet fifth column and the underlying menace of Marxism-Leninism. In any future trials under the Smith Act, the same elaborate business will have to be repeated. This costs huge sums of money and insures long days of wrangling in the courts—all to the benefit and delight of the Communists. It would seem that judicial notice could be taken of the decision of the Supreme Court, and such unnecessary clogging of the administration of justice be avoided.

In the very decision of the Supreme Court on the Smith Act, the Communists received some aid. It lay in Chief Justice Vinson's remark that there are "no absolute truths." This happens to confirm an outstanding feature of the Marxist-Leninist philosophy, even though the Chief Justice clearly did not intend (or perhaps know) that it might be so used. Truth, according to this philosophy, is merely the ideology of the dominant class in any particular period, and this ideology is determined, not by any absolute principle, but by the mode of production and distribution in each era. When the Supreme Court declares that there is no such thing as absolute truth, it unwittingly supplies the Communists with ammunition for their theoretical battles.

The Communists are quick to profit by any expression loosely presented or any technical loopholes which court decisions or legislation happen to offer. This is demonstrated by the careful manner in which they create corporations for each minute division of their movement. The *Freiheit,* a Yiddish-language daily paper, published in New York City, although owned by the party and one of its organs, is incorporated as a separate entity. The *Daily Worker,* operating for years in the same building as the *Freiheit,* and the official daily organ of the party, has long been published by the Freedom of the Press Company, Inc., whose stockholders are supposed to be several gentlewomen of advanced years. This arrangement was set up during the Hitler-Stalin Pact, in order that the *Daily Worker* might make the legal plea that it was distinct from the Communist conspiracy. At the same time, the printing presses of both papers are technically controlled by the F and D Printing Company, another seemingly distinct entity expressly created to do this job. It is completely owned and controlled by the party, but no action against the *Daily Worker* or *Freiheit* is legally possible against the F and D Printing Company.

In the present cold-war crisis, another technique of evasion has been devised. The national headquarters of the Communist Party have been moved from 35 East 12th Street, the building it owns, and where these papers are printed and published. The party has taken offices in Harlem, from which point it can operate underground more efficiently. At the same time, it separates itself physically from the papers, laying the foundation for an additional legal argument that they are not involved in the conspiracy. To add to this fiction, the *Daily Worker* has created still another corporation to replace the Freedom of the Press Company, Inc., and it will now supposedly be the legal entity producing the paper. This will make more difficult any attempt to curb what is, in fact, a telegraph agency for quick communication of directives to the conspirators.

A cry of "freedom of the press" will arise from the fifth column, if any efforts are made to halt this telegraph agency. The cry will be re-echoed in the so-called "liberal" groups, already extensively infiltrated by the Reds, and given to much loose thinking of their own. The cry will have its effect upon the courts unless a more decisive view of the Communist conspiracy is adopted.

The Soviet dictatorship's chief aim is thus being served in America by legal delays and absurd legal fictions. That aim is to preserve a functioning "apparatus" in this country, able to expand its influence and activities through Communist-created or Communist-captured organizations.

The success of the Communists in the courtroom has been offset to some extent by the procedures of Claude B. Cross in the second Hiss trial, by Irving Kaufman in the Rosenberg case, and by the original opinion of Judge Learned Hand on the Smith Act. Such representatives of the Department of Justice as John F. X. McGohey, Irving Saypol, and Thomas Murphy as prosecutors have distinguished themselves by the effective methods they have employed in their examinations. Recently, the deciding opinion by Justice Sherman Minton in upholding New York's Feinberg law has been heartening. But on the whole the course of the law remains uncertain and irregular. The Communists' effort continues to be successful in many instances. That effort is—

through the antics of their lawyers, the cry of civil liberties, and the manipulation of bail—to maintain the life of the conspiracy. In the confusion they cause, we lose sight of their aim to destroy our civil liberties. The defense of American liberty today requires the suppression of its chief enemy, the Red apparatus. But our law still lives largely in another day, and this assures long life to the apparatus. Thus Stalin, with his understanding of an emphasis upon "cadres," triumphs over our less astute and realistic minds.

CHAPTER 5

# Befuddling Us on
# "Peace"

One of the marked features of the testimony of Henry
A. Wallace before the McCarran Committee was his admission that he knew nothing about the Communist
Party line in 1944. It was in the spring of that year that
Mr. Wallace went on his special mission for President
Roosevelt to Soviet Siberia and China. That a leading
official of the United States should set out on such a
serious task without knowing what the Communists were
aiming at seems incredible. And yet that is what the
former Vice President testified.

Even in 1951, Mr. Wallace, by his own statement, did
not know what the Communists had been up to when
he went to Soviet Asia and China. Nevertheless, his
views on Asia upon his return were hailed by the *Daily
Worker* as those of "a great statesman." [1] His pamphlet,
*Our Job in the Pacific*—prepared for the Institute of
Pacific Relations and ghost-written by Mrs. Owen Lattimore—was regarded so highly by Frederick Vanderbilt

[1] The reference to Mr. Wallace as "a great statesman" appeared in the
*Daily Worker* of July 11, 1944, and the extraordinary compliment by
Frederick Vanderbilt Field to the then Vice President is found in the
*Daily Worker* of June 24, 1944.

Field that he placed it alongside Earl Browder's *Teheran* in his *Daily Worker* comments. In addition, the Communists had enthusiastically supported Mr. Wallace for Vice President in 1944 and Secretary of Commerce in 1945, conducting big campaigns on his behalf. Jacques Duclos, the French Communist leader, known as "the voice of Moscow to the West," in demoting Browder had referred to Wallace approvingly as superior in judgment to the former American Communist Party chief. And finally, the Reds rallied to Mr. Wallace as their candidate for President on the ticket of the so-called Progressive Party in 1948. During all this time, according to his own confession, the former Vice President was without information as to Communist intentions.

Lest anyone be inclined to cast too many stones at Mr. Wallace for this ignorance of what he should have known, it can be added that this ignorance was shared by many American leaders in public office, and also many editors. It is because of this that the present phony Communist campaign for "peace" assumes such a threatening aspect. There is no guarantee that American leadership will not be taken in by it—especially since the United States has not insisted that Great Britain withdraw its recognition of Red China. For the chief immediate object of Moscow's "peace drive" is to win universal recognition of Communist control of China, and the seating of Mao Tse-tung in the Security Council of the United Nations.

All through 1951, Red newspapers and periodicals in every country of the world were hammering out Moscow's directives in this campaign for "A Pact of Peace." The Kremlin itself officially suggested such "a pact" to the United States. This government rejected it on the grounds that words were not so necessary as deeds. Nevertheless, the full-dress effort goes on. Every issue of the Cominform's official organ, *For a Lasting Peace, For a People's Democracy,* carries huge front-page headlines: "For a Pact of Peace!" Every issue contains articles supporting that slogan and giving instructions as to how it can be advanced in various countries.

The character of the proposal is obvious in the fact that one of the chief signatories to the "pact" would be Red China. With that act—in itself a recognition of the Communist regime—would go the seating of a Red China representative on the Security Council, the withdrawal of United Nations troops from Korea, an abandonment of any plan to arm Japan, and most recently the proposal to "unify" Germany on terms favorable to Soviet ambitions. All these provisions are included in the proposal; they are the essence of the "pact." They represent a complete surrender to the Kremlin.

This campaign, pushed with vigor by the Reds everywhere, is only the most recent of a series of "peace offensives" by the Kremlin since 1947, when the Information Bureau of the Communist Party, known as the Cominform, was established. It was the late A. Zhdanov, then the leading figure in Soviet Russia next to Stalin, who first called for such an "offensive." The American Communists responded promptly, and they have been in step with each of the subsequent crusades as they were developed by the Kremlin.

These Communist "peace offensives," designed to befuddle American opinion and disarm and defeat the United States, have been more successful than is generally imagined. They have been supported by many prominent men and women—professors and teachers, scientists, clergymen, lawyers, artists, writers, actors, and professional people in many other fields. These prominent people infect others. They influence newspapers of large circulation. Their influence extends far out into the American community, causing bewilderment and hesitation at best, and at worst organized aid to Soviet aggression. They contribute to the general vacillation which has marked American policy.

Testimony to the impact of these labors was given by General MacArthur in his address last fall to the American Legion Convention at Miami. The former commander of the Pacific charged that the State Department was about to recognize Red China when his "cease fire" offer in Korea halted them. Such recognition would have been a gigantic victory for the Kremlin. The Communist international conspiracy has constantly emphasized to its followers the vital place of China in the Soviet plan for world conquest. "The road to Paris is through Peiping" is an old Red adage. A reading of the files of the *Communist International* magazine, the *New Times* of Moscow, and the Cominform's present organ, will show how central this conception is.

There has been a denial of MacArthur's charge, but corroboration for his statement comes from a number of sources. The *Pathfinder,* a magazine of national information, published an interview with Dr. Jessup on September 21, 1949, concerning the Far East. Jessup was reported as favoring recognition of Communist China, "provided she respects existing treaties like that which guarantees the security of the British colony in Hong Kong." Further corroboration is found in Secretary of State Dean Acheson's omission, prior to the Korean aggression by the Communists, of Formosa and Korea from the American line of defense in the Far East. We now know that influential experts of the IPR recommended that the United States get Great Britain to do the job of recognizing Mao Tse-tung, and the failure of the State Department to insist upon the withdrawal of such recognition looks the same way. The *White Paper,* edited by Jessup for the State Department, comes in with its condemnation of the Chinese Nationalists and its apology for American official complacency toward the Chinese Reds.

Many sponsors of the Communist "peace" front are of a character to inspire respect in certain official circles in Washington, because of past connections there. One of them was Dr. Robert Morss Lovett, formerly of the University of Chicago and secretary of the Virgin Islands during the Roosevelt Administration. Lovett has been a member, incidentally, of more than eighty Communist fronts. Another person of influence, because of her interest in social legislation, is Mary Van Kleeck, formerly an official of the Russell Sage Foundation—a member of approximately sixty Communist fronts during every twist and turn of the party line. Another is Corliss Lamont, millionaire heir of the late senior member of the banking house of J. P. Morgan. Lamont has sponsored or joined some fifty Communist fronts, and was connected with the IPR. There are scores of such names, including Carey McWilliams of the *Nation,* Dr. Henry Pratt Fairchild of New York University, and Jack R. McMichael, secretary of the Methodist Federation for Social Action. McWilliams and Fairchild have been connected with about fifty Red-sponsored organizations; McMichael with thirty.

The Soviet "peace offensive" was set into action by the National Council of the Arts, Sciences, and Professions, the Communist-front organization calculated to have the greatest influence in the national capital. It was a continuation of the Independent Citizens Committee of the Arts, Sciences, and Professions which had been so prominent in the 1944 national election. Under the chairmanship of the late Jo Davidson, the sculptor, this organization had won the admiration and respect of many political leaders. In 1949, following Moscow's order that the intellectuals of the world be rallied to Stalin's aims, it joined the movement for a World Congress of Intellectuals. A delegate to this Congress, Dr. Bryn J. Hovde, then head of the New School for Social Research, wrote of the meeting: "Every speech insulting the United States and glorifying the Soviets was wildly applauded." Stirring up the delegates to hatred of the United States, the representative of the Soviet Union, Alexander Fadayev, compared those writers and artists who favored the United States to "jackals" and "hyenas." He denounced the United States in intemperate language as the conspirator and organizer of a new war.

Among those "American delegates" who went along with Fadayev were Howard Fast, novelist, who has now acknowledged that he is a Communist; Norman Corwin, prominent script writer for radio and television; Albert E. Kahn, author; Donald Ogden Stewart, script writer for the motion picture industry; Clifford Durr, former member of the Federal Communications Commission, an active official of the National Lawyers Guild. Dr. Hovde's pleas for "democracy as the only basis for peace," he tells us, got a cold shoulder from all these people.

The message of the World Congress was brought to the United States in a conference held at the Waldorf-Astoria Hotel in New York City in March, 1949. This was the so-called Scientific and Cultural Conference for World Peace, arranged by the National Council of the Arts, Sciences, and Professions. An unpublicized but prominent participant in this conference, of course, was Alexander Trachtenberg, Moscow's commissar for culture in the United States and one of the twenty-one Red leaders indicted in 1951. Trachtenberg has had a hand in every subversive move made by the Communists in the American intellectual world. All the assaults upon the United States made at the World Congress were repeated and re-emphasized at this conference. Richard Boyer, frequent contributor to the *New Yorker,* announced openly that he was a member of the Communist Party and as such called for civil disobedience to American authorities. Clifford Odets, the playwright, declared that "one of the greatest frauds ever perpetrated" was "the fraud that the Soviet Union is making a war against the United States." To this he added: "As an American, in the tradition of the American artists of the past, the moral values of my world are in question, not Russia's."

The Waldorf-Astoria conference called for promotion of Soviet Russia's foreign policy and for the rallying of American professionals behind such a program even to the point of civil disobedience to the American government. From then on, very special attention was given to work among the scientists, already well begun by the party. This endeavor finally reached such high importance that at the Fifteenth National Convention of the Communist Party, held secretly in December, 1950, certain scientists were singled out for official praise by the party for their labors "in the cause of peace." These men included Linus C. Pauling, head of the chemistry division of the California Institute of Technology, Harlow Shapley, astronomer, of Harvard University, Kirtley Mather of the same institution, Anton J. Carlson of the University of Chicago, Philip Morrison of Cornell, and Dirk

Struik of the Massachusetts Institute of Technology. Since that time, one of these men, Dr. Struik, has been indicted in Massachusetts for conspiratorial activities. The open praise of these men of science by a Soviet conspiracy at a time of Soviet aggression is significant. It does not indicate, of course, that subversion is a rule among American scientists. But it does point to a militant and organized minority which is busy on behalf of Stalin, and in a position to do great harm to American security. The almost unprecedented hailing of these men in proceedings which were later published (in the February, 1951, issue of *Political Affairs*) had a twofold purpose: To enlist lesser scientists in the conspiracy by the use of these influential names, and to persuade some of these lesser scientists to engage in espionage as well as infiltration. From the record, as established by official American hearings and documents, the maneuver was successful. The cases of Dr. Clarence Hiskey and of the Rosenbergs are illustrations of the party's success in penetrating sensitive laboratories and industries through the help of scientific workers.

From the Waldorf-Astoria conference to the end of 1951, a succession of organizations was created by the Reds to ballyhoo Soviet Russia's "peace" crusades. No less than seven of these organizations appeared on the scene, bearing different names but with the same basic personnel in the sponsoring lists. This rapid change of titles for substantially the same groups is an old Communist device, designed to confuse the public mind and make it possible to lure a constant stream of new people into the "movement."

The directing head of these shifting efforts was, and is, the World Peace Council, brought into existence at the second World Peace Congress in November, 1950.

Veterans of the American Red fronts sponsored this Congress, and appeared among the membership of the council itself. Among them were the Reverend Joseph Fletcher, Paul Robeson, Howard Fast, Dr. W. E. B. DuBois, and Charles Howard, a lawyer of Iowa. The real direction continued to come from the Cominform, which in each issue of its official organ hammered home the necessity of spreading this work far and wide. The American Communist Party gave orders for a total mobilization to make all these "peace" moves a success.

American cities and the countryside were flooded with petitions, first for the Stockholm Peace Petition of 1950, then for the "Peace Information Center," and then in 1951 for the "Pact of Peace." The first appeal was cleverly addressed to "all men and women of good will throughout the world." It followed exactly the demands of the Soviet Government for "the outlawing of atomic weapons as instruments of aggression and mass murder of peoples." Its effect, naturally, would have been to render the Western world helpless by persuading it to end the manufacture of atomic bombs, while Soviet Russia would be bound by no such limitation. This was made doubly ironic by the Kremlin's simultaneous refusal to join with the United States and other nations in turning over all atomic materials and information to the control of the United Nations. Even the imprudence of this proposal so far as concerned American security, seeing that the United States had the advantage of Russia both in know-how and equipment, did not lead Stalin and his associates to accept it. The spirit of the Stockholm Petition was made perfectly clear at the conference in Stockholm which issued it. Attacks upon the United States were a prominent feature of the meeting, and were participated in by an American Communist Party member, Albert E. Kahn, who joined his bitter slanders against the American Republic with fulsome praise of the Soviet Russia. The hand of Moscow was thus openly shown as controlling the conference, although when the carefully worded petition came out, no one could ever have guessed it.

Knowing the solicitude of mothers for their sons in the armed forces, the Reds have put special emphasis on this theme. This is a repetition of what was done among women during the period of the Hitler-Stalin Pact, when the Kremlin was allied with the Nazi dictator. At that time the Cominform inspired the Red-controlled executive committee of the Women's International Democratic Federation to issue an "Appeal to Women of the World." This occurred in August, 1951, and the burden of its message is contained in this prominent sentence:

Anguished mothers ask themselves—how can war be avoided? Must ruin and suffering spread to the entire world? "We demand the conclusion of a Pact of Peace among the five Great Powers: The United States of America, the Soviet Union, the Chinese People's Republic, Great Britain, and France. . . . We shall consider the refusal by the government of any of the Great Powers to meet for the conclusion of such a pact as evidence of aggressive designs on the part of that government. We call upon all peace-loving nations to support the demand for a Pact of Peace which shall be open to all countries.

A detailed program was issued for the infiltration of women's groups. This recommended the use of "all forms of graphic, press, and oral propaganda" which would include "radio, the circulation of handbills and pamphlets, speeches at meetings, talks with small groups of women, and private conversations with women at their homes and places of employment." These efforts were directed toward "exposing the lies and slanders spread by the warmongers." Signature campaigns were to be started all over again, and "protest meetings" organized against the "reactionaries" and against "repression of the fighters for peace." This last phrase referred to the trials of Communists for conspiracy to overthrow the government, and meant that a cry should be raised that these conspirators were being "persecuted" as "advocates of peace."

In the United States the Communists and their allies immediately swung into action with new signature efforts among women. A huge propaganda campaign was launched which asserted that the four Communists who outraged American justice by jumping bail after conviction had been "framed" for their devotion to "peace." When Gus Hall, leading Communist organizer, was arrested in Mexico City as a fugitive from justice, a unanimous cry went up from the Communists and their friends that he was a martyr to the cause of "peace." This was made the subject of a flood of Red demands upon the United States Supreme Court that it give a rehearing quite without precedent to the Communist lawyers who had been found guilty of contempt for their hoodlum tactics at the trial at Foley Square in New York before Judge Harold Medina. When the rehearing was actually granted on a small technical point, the *Daily Worker* ascribed this to "popular indignation"—which always means the "indignation" worked up by the Communists and their allies.

The Communist organ boasted that "the pressure of the people" may still induce the Supreme Court to nullify "the savage jail sentence against the Foley Square lawyers." In this case their boast was vain.

Together with their attempt to subvert women, and

particularly mothers, the Communists, who are atheistic, used the cloak of religion to forward their propaganda. In mid-1951 there occurred "interfaith conferences and meetings for peace," the sponsors of which were persons long connected with Communist fronts. Executive director of this "interfaith" maneuver is Dr. Willard Uphaus, a Protestant minister recently discharged as executive secretary of the National Religion and Labor Foundation of New Haven, Connecticut, because of his pro-Communist tendencies. Uphaus attended the so-called "Second World Peace Congress," and was prominent there in assailing the United States. From there he went to the Soviet capital as the guest of the Russian delegation, and returned declaring Soviet Russia to be a citadel of "peace." Other sponsors known now as Red-fronters are Mary Van Kleeck and the Reverend Joseph Fletcher of the Episcopal Theological School at Cambridge, Massachusetts.

In connection with these larger meetings, smaller conferences, particularly of women, were called in local communities. These "interfaith" gatherings always ended up with the circulation of petitions for the Pact of Peace. Many women signed these petitions, totally unaware of their Red origin, or of the fact that by their signatures they were demanding the recognition of Red China. How badly they were taken in was made clear by the exchange of greetings between Mao Tse-tung, the Communist Chinese leader, and Joseph Stalin, which took place at the same time the petitions were being circulated. In this interchange, Mao Tse-tung declared officially the solidarity of the Chinese Reds with the Soviet dictator, and pledged war to the death against "American imperialism." Simultaneously, this adherence to the Kremlin was being announced throughout the whole Communist

Party structure in China. Thus we read in the Cominform's organ for September 28, 1951, that Tung Pi-wu, member of the Political Bureau of the Chinese Communist Party, declared: "The Chinese people stand firmly in the world camp of peace and democracy headed by the Soviet Union, and will strive to the end in order to smash the aggressive war plot of the imperialist camp headed by American imperialism."

This use of "religion" as a cover for Red subversion through front groups is not entirely new, although it is now being resorted to on a larger scale than before. For some years, J. Edgar Hoover, of the Federal Bureau of Investigation, and the House Committee on Un-American Activities have warned about the continuous sponsorship of Red-created committees by certain Protestant ministers. While a very small group compared to the loyal thousands in the ministry, these men have the advantage of being aggressive, concealed, and working together behind the scenes. Some of them have advanced considerably in influence during their Red-front careers. A striking illustration is the Reverend John B. Thompson, who was a rather obscure minister in Tulsa, Oklahoma, when in 1941 he was chosen chairman of the American Peace Mobilization, dedicated to aiding Hitler and attacking President Roosevelt. Today, he has advanced to the position of Dean of the Rockefeller Chapel at the University of Chicago, where he is in a position to affect the morale of many young men going into military service. In May, 1950, he turned up as an initiating sponsor of the Communist-organized Mid-Century Conference for Peace, serving as chairman of one of its chief panel discussions, and opening the principal session with an account of the history of the congress.

The Right Reverend Arthur W. Moulton, Protestant

Episcopal Bishop of Utah (retired), is another who has lent his name extensively to Stalinist "peace causes." He was co-chairman back in 1949 of the American Sponsoring Committee for the World Peace Congress, and thereafter associated himself actively with successive ventures of the same kind. All in all, he has been a member or sponsor of at least ten Communist fronts. These services were recognized by Moscow in 1951 when Bishop Moulton was named one of the few recipients throughout the world of the Stalin Peace Prize. With his name can be linked that of Dr. Harry F. Ward, retired professor of Christian Ethics at Union Theological Seminary, who has always been an eager participant in these Communist endeavors. Dr. Ward, in addition to his recent services to the "peace" groups, has been a member all told of sixty Communist fronts.

These men, and a number like them, have much influence among the various religious denominations upon both ministers and laymen. These, in turn, affect the opinion of wider groups in their community or state, and even throughout the nation. Their pressure is felt by men running for public office, and is registered in the vacillations and tragic blunders of American foreign policy.

A like influence is exercised by men and women connected with our great organs of public opinion. It is no light matter that Olin Downes, music critic of the New York *Times*, and a person of considerable standing on that paper, was a prominent sponsor of the first Stalinist world peace congress. He was also actively identified with the Waldorf-Astoria conference, and has been a sponsor or member of at least twenty-five Communist fronts. Downes has not satisfied himself with merely lending his name, but has served as a panel chairman and also as a panel speaker at these "peace" conferences. Even more serious was the identification, by five witnesses before the McCarran Subcommittee, of Joseph Barnes, former foreign editor of the New York *Herald-Tribune* and a power in that paper, as a Communist. Barnes has recently been made a vice president of the publishing house of Simon and Schuster. His influence has been, and remains, enormous. There is also Robert M. Coates, well-known art critic and contributor to the *New Yorker,* a member of ten Communist fronts, who has given open support to party candidates in election campaigns. And, of course, Norman Corwin, previously mentioned as a radio-television writer, who was an enthusiastic delegate to the Waldorf-Astoria conference, and whose program the *Daily Worker* supports with real fervor.

These are just samples of the names of public opinion makers that could be listed to explain why such confusion about Soviet Russia and its designs creeps into the press, radio, television, and other communication media in regard to Soviet Russia and its designs.

The "prominent personalities," and others not so prominent but more active, who co-operate with the Communist conspiracy, are not content with lending their names. Nor do they stop, as a rule, with conspicuous attendance at conferences and rallies. Most of them seek to forward the Stalinist game in other ways. There is the case of I. F. Stone, columnist for the New York *Daily Compass,* who at the Waldorf-Astoria conference denounced "the machinery of the American government" as "set for war." He has asserted a number of times that all the Soviet peace efforts have been rejected by the United States.

Rose Russell, chief executive of the New York Teachers Union, has also given dynamic assistance to schemes of the Communist conspiracy. She stood out as a sponsor of the first World Peace Congress, called under Moscow auspices in Paris in 1949. She has been prominent in the Congress of American Women, a Red-created group, and in its parent body, the Women's International Democratic Federation. Nor was she just a name on a letterhead; she played a directive role in obtaining signatures among professional people for the Stockholm Peace Petition. Successor to Dr. Bella Dodd, who left her post in the Teachers' Union to become legislative representative of the Communist Party in New York State, Miss Russell directed the teachers' body so carefully along the Communist Party line that it was finally denied representation before the Board of Education. The wide extent of her influence is shown by the fact that, while engaged in these activities, she was granted a special award on a television program "for her outstanding work in education."

Another person who combines the sponsorship of Red fronts with widespread activity on behalf of Stalinist causes is Arthur Osman, president of the Distributive, Processing, and Office Workers Union, an organization recently formed from a merger of three Red-ruled unions expelled from the CIO. Before a Madison Square Garden rally of the Union's members on October 23, 1951, Osman urged incessant work in behalf of the Moscow "peace" proposals. In the Labor Peace Conference, a highly advertised meeting of three hundred shop stewards organized by Stalinists, Osman played an active role. He went so far in his devotion to the cause as to supply the union hall on Astor Place, New York, for a meeting of Red delegates to promote the *Daily Worker* in 1945.

Thus through discipline and influence, the party sees

to it that both Communists and fellow travelers in front groups function in its behalf. Having policies tailor-made for them by Moscow, they are able to concentrate on carrying out orders, and can each perform the work of several thinking men. Placed in a key spot, the Red or fellow traveler can move thousands of non-Communists into action for some "immediate demand" that is linked up with the current purposes of the Soviet dictatorship. These thousands will serve Stalin without having the slightest idea what it is all about.

In these ways, the conferences staged by Moscow on behalf of "peace" have been a substantial contribution toward befuddling American opinion, causing a vacillating foreign policy, and aiding Soviet aggression. The Cominform, in its organ of December 7, 1951, notes with satisfaction the progress of the "peace movement in the United States." It calls the roll of various Communist fronts and describes what they are achieving. Among these comments we note:

The *Daily Worker* reports that the American Peace Crusade National Committee has undertaken to get 1,000,000 signatures to a petition calling for a Great Power conference to settle their differences and sign a peace pact.

Again:

Four hundred and seventeen prominent public, labor, and religious leaders, including the heads of three theological schools and representatives of different religious bodies from forty-three states, addressed a letter to President Truman urging that he exert a supreme effort "to bring the fighting in Korea to an end and to achieve a truce that will lead to the full restoration of peace."

Among those reported as signing the letter are Professor Emily Greene Balch, who has been a member of many Communist fronts, John Long, president of the Southern Christian Institute, Pat Rice, president of Local 600, United Automobile Workers Union, Professor Robert Havighurst of the University of Chicago, and James Wolfe, Justice of the Supreme Court of Utah, who has likewise sponsored many Red fronts.

The Cominform organ further observes: "The sentiments of many Americans are also reflected in the numerous letters sent to American newspapers," a device at which the Communists and those sympathetic to them are expert and assiduous.

In the pages of the same organ we read constant expressions of loyalty from the Communist leaders in all countries to "our liberator, the great Soviet Union," and declarations of fidelity to "proletarian internationalism and socialism, to our leader and teacher, the great Stalin." This was the phrase used by Vladimir Poptomov, speaking for the Politburo of the Communist Party of Bulgaria, where the Red terror rages. Another Red spokesman pledges adherence "to the banner of Marx, Engels, Lenin, and Stalin, and to the triumph of Communism throughout the world." K. E. Voroshilov, representing the Moscow Politburo, at the August, 1951, celebration of the "liberation of Rumania," is quoted as concluding his address with the ejaculation: "Glory to the great leader and teacher of all progressive mankind, the best friend of the Roumanian people and the working people all over the world, our Stalin!" And it is set down that these words were greeted by "loud cheers in honor of the great friend of the Rumanian people and the peoples of the world, Comrade J. V. Stalin."

The determination revealed in these pledges to make Stalin and the men in the Kremlin rulers of the world, is the real motive and meaning of all the talk about "peace." The blinding of a section of the American nation to these pledges and this determination, by drawing over it the mantle of devotion to peace, is of great help to Stalin in his triumphal march of conquest.

On November 2, 1951, the *United States News and World Report,* a national weekly news magazine, published a feature editorial declaring that Soviet Russia was winning World War III with ease. The survey made by that publication showed that while the United States has been preparing for some eventual future military attack by Soviet Russia, Stalin has been waging the war since 1945 and winning it. Some 600,000,000 people have been brought under his rule in the course of five years, and the fate of other hundreds of millions hangs perilously in the balance. In Asia the way has been cleared for a conquest of India, Indo-China, Burma, and Indonesia. In Europe powerful fifth columns are active in the very countries the United States is arming to halt future aggression.

The greatest conquest in the history of the world had been achieved. It was achieved, this survey reported, by a nation infinitely weaker than the United States, both economically and militarily. Our nation has been frittering away its strength in a bewildered, blundering policy while the Kremlin knows its goal and goes toward it step by step.

These extreme statements are confirmed by the realities of the present world scene. The United States has been unable to wage a war in Korea which would bring the Communist aggression to its knees and unify the country —the only permanent solution. It has passed the banner of German unification into Soviet hands, while hesitating to rearm West Germany. The Marshall Plan has been of temporary aid in rebuilding the economies of Western

Europe—except for Great Britain—but has not been able to snuff out the Soviet fifth columns. The Italian Communists were stunningly defeated before the Marshall Plan went into effect, but staunchly held their own in the 1951 election. No hope has been held out to the underground movements in the satellite countries; the flouting of the Atlantic Charter in their subjection has not even been brought effectually to the floor of the United Nations. Help to the guerrillas in China or the underground in East Europe has received but slight consideration. Those who should be our allies have been left to the mercy of the Soviet conquerors.

These staggering victories of a comparatively weak Soviet Russia over the powerful United States cannot be ascribed entirely to Communist "peace" moves and other intrigues. They arise partly from the reluctance of the American nation to understand the true nature of Soviet Communism, and its intrinsic need for world conquest. This stems in part from Anglophile sentiments in certain sections, a tendency to applaud everything that Great Britain does, such as recognition of Red China. It stems also from the sudden emergence of the United States as a dominant world power, without sufficient knowledge, or experience, or even a habit of studying the enemy. The Kremlin is constantly telling its followers, through directives translated into English and easily available, what it plans to do. But these sources seem a closed book to most Americans, even those charged with the leadership of public opinion. Any continued examination of the Cominform's organ, *For a Lasting Peace, For a People's Democracy*, would uncover repeated statements that Stalin is the "leader and guide" of the peoples of the world, that is, their would-be conqueror. It would also reveal the changing orders he gives to his fifth columns, and thus keep our leadership forewarned of what is coming.

But into the midst of this general ignorance and ineptitude in foreign affairs, the phony "peace" offensives depicted in this chapter bring additional confusion. They add to the uncertainty in the American mind. They extend out into circles of wealth and influence, into every conceivable area of opinion, making vacillations more permanent and paralyzing the national will. People bewildered by these offensives encourage our leadership in halting measures, half-hearted proposals, and thus forestall the one thing that the crisis demands if the free world is to survive—a firm stand against Soviet aggression everywhere.

# CHAPTER 6

# *Smearing the Ex-Communists*

If the Communist conspiracy wishes to obscure its real purpose of destroying the United States government as it ardently desires to do, it is logical that much of its energy will be devoted to destroying those who formerly were Communists or fellow travelers and have now publicly renounced their adherence to this aim. Because they know from direct and personal experience that Communism would smash the last vestige of freedom in America, they constitute the chief threat to the conspiracy. They are perfectly acquainted, as few others are, with the literature, directives, and purposes of the Soviet fifth column. It is precisely on these subjects that the American people most need information, and which they most sadly lack.

It is not surprising that the conspiracy does all in its power to advance a "smear campaign" against those ex-Communists who speak out against it and who are in fact required, under subpoena, to testify in courts or before Congressional committees. Just as gangsters kill off those who leave their ranks, so the gangster-like Communist organization resorts to every method of vilification to discredit those who turn against it. On the other hand, of course, there is nothing the Communists will not do, no hand they will not shake, in behalf of one of their own.

For example, the Australian-born alien, Harry Renton Bridges, in October, 1951, took the lead in organizing a conference in New York City of all the unions which had been expelled from the CIO because they were Communist-controlled. Although the meeting was carefully guarded to prevent intrusion, with the radio blaring in the conference room to drown out any sounds of the discussions of newspaper men or government agents on the outside, enough came out in statements by Bridges himself to indicate its purpose. Preparing for a nation-wide attack on what was called "the wage freeze," the leaders of these unions laid their plans for disrupting the American economy. Consolidation of their efforts could prove one of the most valuable contributions to Stalin's plan. Paralysis of production has always been a chief item in the Communist strategy of conquest.

Bridges' leading role in this new endeavor is all the more striking because his freedom to act in the United States has been made possible by government officials and agencies. On December 28, 1939, Dean James M. Landis of the Harvard Law School, presiding for the government, declared Bridges not to be a Communist. Again, on January 3, 1942, after a second hearing on Bridges' deportation, the Board of Immigration Appeals in San Francisco upheld that finding.

Three years later, in renewed proceedings against Bridges, the United States Supreme Court, by a vote of five to three, put their stamp of approval on him as a non-Red. The late Justice Frank Murphy, in writing the decision for the majority report, declared that "the

Bridges case would stand forever as a monument of man's intolerance to man."

In each of these cases, the Red uproar in defense of Bridges, which was loud and nationwide, centered around character assassination of the ex-Communists who testified for the government under subpoena. Each of the witnesses against Bridges in the Landis proceedings was assailed as despicable, immoral, also as a psychopathic liar and unworthy of belief. The terms "renegade," "labor spy," "spy for the Hearst press," "labor disrupter," and other epithets of a more vicious character were hurled at Benjamin Gitlow, former general secretary of the Communist Party; Howard Rushmore, who was once employed on the *Daily Worker;* Nat Honig, former friend of William Z. Foster; and Harry Lundeberg, secretary-treasurer of the Sailors Union of the Pacific.

These Communist smears were accepted at face value by Dean Landis. Of some of the ex-Communists called upon by the government in the case before him, Landis stated in his official report:

Of witness Leech: "[Candor and a modicum of coherence] were absent with regard to Leech."

Of witness Knowles: "He was neither a candid nor a forthright witness."

Of witness Humphreys: ". . . whose tendency toward prevarication was almost pathological."

Several other ex-Communists who were government witnesses got the same treatment from Landis, and he summed up his view of all of them by declaring their testimony "a morass of prevarication." To Bridges, on the other hand, Landis paid the warmest compliments for his "fighting apologia" from the witness stand.[1]

[1] These excerpts from Dean Landis' comments were reprinted with warm approval by the *Daily Worker* of May 29, 1942.

Today, Dean Landis' views on these ex-Communists and on Bridges have been revealed as thoroughly false. In 1950 such authoritative witnesses as Mervyn Rathborne, former Communist and head of the Communist-dominated American Communications Association, Lew Michener, who had directed the North American Aircraft strike for the Communists during the Hitler-Stalin Pact period, and Manning Johnson, Negro trade unionist and former member of the National Committee of the Communist Party, were among the witnesses confirming his Communist affiliations. It is significant that Dean Landis, although he officially injured the reputations of the ex-Communist witnesses who are now proved to be right, has never apologized for his false judgment. The smear he implanted against them remains, undenied, on the record.

The peculiar tendency of Dean Landis, now a high government official, to agree with the Red smear, is noteworthy in view of the fact that Federal Judge Charles B. Sears had overruled further rehearings before the Board of Immigration Appeal, which vied with Landis in echoing the Communist assault on the ex-Reds. Of Harry Lundeberg, for instance, although he was a well-known labor leader, the four-man board declared him to be "admittedly a biased witness," and one who "impresses neither in truthfulness nor in forthrightness." Others were subject to even more vilification.

To all this was added the defense of Bridges by Frances Perkins, then Secretary of Labor. She officially declared the Landis decision to be flawless, said that Bridges was innocent of any Red taint, and assailed those who testified against him as stool pigeons. Miss Perkins, now a member of the United States Civil Service Commission, has not apologized to those anti-Communists she recklessly attacked when she spoke out in defense of Harry Bridges.

How grievously Miss Perkins, Dean Landis, the board of appeals, and Justice Murphy's decision deceived the American people is evident from an examination of the career of Harry Bridges. In a number of proceedings witnesses have shown that he directed the infiltration of Hawaii, key to American defense in the Pacific, particularly through the chief Communist agent there, Jack Hall. This infiltration has been disclosed as part of a general Communist plan to make the Pacific islands part of the Soviet empire as a base from which to smash "American imperialism." With such a record, Bridges operates today as American representative of the World Federation of Trade Unions, as head of its maritime division. This federation, through its officers, has declared Stalin's Russia to be the model for all other countries and the one place on earth where workers are emancipated.

From these episodes it is clear that the success of the conspiracy's character assassination against ex-Communists depends upon enlisting the aid of non-Communist individuals and information media. It is a standard Communist tactic to have the scurrilous expressions that first appear in the *Daily Worker* spread first by the concealed Communists and then picked up by non-Communists. If certain government officials so readily absorb these slanders and make them their own, as the Bridges case indicates so eloquently, then many others will do the same. The cruelest injustice has thereby been perpetrated against former members of the conspiracy who have sought to make amends for their past conduct by telling the truth to the Federal Bureau of Investigation and the Department of Justice. The United States has, in consequence, lost many witnesses who could have been of great value against the conspiracy. They have been the ex-Communists who have sneaked out of the party without making any contribution to American security and who are free from criticism. The number of those who are willing to testify against the conspiracy is rapidly diminishing, and with good reason.

Consider the ex-Communist who studies the case of John Leech, one of the witnesses against Bridges who received such a violent verbal assault from Dean Landis. His fate warns every ex-Communist (unless, as a friend of mine put it, "he is either a hero or a fool") against giving information to the FBI or participating in any trial involving the Red conspiracy. Leech was a section organizer of the Communist Party in a very important spot, that portion of California which covers Hollywood. In 1939, he left the Communist conspiracy and was subpoenaed before the House Committee on Un-American Activities. There, under oath, he exposed the extent of Red infiltration into the motion-picture colony, naming Frank Tuttle and a number of other prominent directors, writers, and artists as Reds. For this he was subjected to the utmost persecution, the Communists beginning it and non-Communists continuing it. This was so effective that finally all employment was denied to him and he was literally starving. When he did occasionally obtain a job, it was not long until the whispering campaign followed him, and he was again out of work. This continued for years.

In 1951, Frank Tuttle himself acknowledged under oath that he had been a Communist when Leech identified him as such. Before the House Committee on Un-American Activities, testimony was given by witness after witness confirming almost word-for-word what Leech had stated twelve years before.

Another victim of character assassination is George Hewitt, Negro ex-Communist of New York. Entering the Red ranks when a comparatively young man, Hewitt had been sent to the Lenin School in Moscow and had later served the Communist Party for a number of years as section organizer in Harlem. There he was known under the party name of Tim Holmes. Breaking with the conspiracy in 1944, he was subpoenaed repeatedly a few years later by the Department of Justice, and specifically by its Immigration Division, for testimony in cases affecting alien Communists.

Immediately there began for him a reign of terror that never let up. Living in an area where the Communists were strongly entrenched, and finding it difficult to move (particularly by reason of his race), he and his family were subjected to many indignities. Obscene phrases were written on his door, constant threats were made against him, and his children were annoyed whenever they appeared on the streets. The strain upon him proved too much, and in a hearing for the Immigration Division in Cleveland, he suffered a stroke which has left him a cripple. He was only in his mid-forties when this occurred.

Communist wrath has also been vented on the head of Joseph Kornfeder, originally known under the party name of Joseph Zack. After years as a member of the highest commissions in the conspiracy, during which he made several visits to Moscow and attended the Lenin School, Kornfeder left the Communist Party in 1934. Twelve years later, the government began to call upon him as a witness, and he proved to be valuable in a number of important trials and deportation cases. The usual chorus of abuse was hurled at him by the Reds—"renegade," "informer," and "police spy." But he was specifically accused, since the Communists must always show some ulterior motive in those who actually break with them, of testifying solely for the twenty-five dollars a day which he occasionally received for his service. This petty sum, despite the physical strain and financial losses in attending hearings or trials, was magnified into a source of livelihood. As always, this did not remain exclusively a Red charge; it extended beyond the pages of the *Daily Worker* to be taken up by non-Communist individuals and publications. This reached such a point in the summer of 1950 that the *Washington Post,* which has been a stronghold of appeasement of the Reds, directly charged Kornfeder with having financial rewards as his motive in testifying at the hearing of eight teachers before the Board of Education in New York. These teachers, associated with the Teachers Union, had been charged with insubordination for refusing to state whether or not they were members of the Communist Party. The *Washington Post's* accusation was met by a sharp threat of action on Kornfeder's part, and the newspaper abandoned its campaign of vilification. But much of the damage had been done, and the campaign against this valuable witness for the government continues.

In the 1951 hearings before the Subversive Activities Control Board, appointed by President Truman under the McCarran Act, the lawyers for the Communist Party went to unusual lengths in their attack on Kornfeder. So vicious were Vito Marcantonio and his associates in their examination that Kornfeder refused to testify further if these smear methods were permitted. The presiding chairman of the hearing, former Representative Charles La-Follette, who had been extremely lenient with the counsel for the Reds, was so determined that Kornfeder should be subjected to this form of examination that he threatened to resign if it was prohibited. Although LaFollette

later withdrew his resignation, his act is a symbol of the
extraordinary privileges enjoyed by lawyers for the Communists in building up the Red smear campaigns in the
courtroom. None of these efforts has ever impeached or
discredited a witness for the government in recent years,
and the sole purpose for their introduction in the various trials and hearings is to lay the foundation for a
scurrilous drive of intimidation outside the courtroom.
It must be stated that under the new chairman of the
Subversive Activities Control Board, Peter Campbell
Brown, these Communist tactics have been checked, and
a judicial atmosphere has been introduced into the proceedings.

Chief targets of the Red smear have been Whittaker
Chambers, Elizabeth Bentley, and me. Every epithet and
charge in the wide range of Communist vilification has
been employed against this trio. The cause for this concentration is readily understandable; we three have
touched the very heart of the conspiracy in the testimony elicited from us under subpoena of Congressional
committees and the courts. We have focussed the search-
light on the treasures of the conspiracy—the concealed
Communists and their close allies. The October 1, 1951,
issue of the *Daily Worker* devotes a full-column editorial
to assailing the three of us and our "well-paid, lying fantasies." These are fictions which the Communists have to
resurrect continuously. We find them as far back as 1946
in a pamphlet issued by Gerhart Eisler. He had been
named by me as the representative of the Communist
International in this country, functioning under cover.
The pamphlet was issued in connection with that charge
and was entitled, *Eisler Strikes Back—My Reply to Budenz.*
In its pages he not only referred to me as "a rat" for

whom he would later send the rat-catchers, but he also declared my motive was "Judas gold."

Accompanying these and other invectives was Eisler's assertion that he was not a leading Communist but a refugee from Nazism. Recent history has disclosed who was the Ananias in that case. The Red conspiracy went to great lengths to assure Eisler's escape from this country on the Polish ship, *Batory*. Immediately upon his safe arrival in Germany, a refugee from American justice, he was made propaganda minister of the Soviet-occupied region in Germany, a member of the national council governing that area, and a professor of the University of Leipzig. That reveals what a very important person he was, and confirms the facts brought out in the testimony at his two trials in Washington in which he was convicted. Among those appearing as witnesses against him was his sister, Ruth Fischer, who told of his widespread activities in Germany and China as a Red leader. She disclosed also that in China he, as a representative of the Communist International, had been responsible for the purging of many connected with the Red Chinese apparatus.

But the sad thing for the American republic was that his self-defense and invectives, part of an intensive campaign for his defense, caused a large number of men and women of influence to defend him. Through their pressure, at least in part, he was permitted his freedom while appeals in his cases were pending in the United States Supreme Court, and this enabled him to escape—to become one of this nation's most alert enemies on the European continent.

It is in this ability to get others, who are non-Communists or thought to be non-Communists, to take up the vituperation first uttered by the Red organs that Stalin's aims have been greatly furthered in this country. Just as in the propaganda against "the second imperialist war" during the Hitler-Stalin period and in the "peace crusades" of the present, the wave of Red-created phrases travels into non-Communist territory and is found in the writings or other utterances of those not directly connected with the conspiracy. By constant repetition and by "getting the word around," an atmosphere is created which encourages non-Communists to assault those ex-Reds who respond to government subpoena against the conspiracy. These assaults are made despite the fact that those who make them, often in high positions, must be aware that a court order in the form of a subpoena cannot be ignored by any responsible citizen. What these attacks are actually recommending is either defiance of the courts or perjury on behalf of the Red conspiracy and its friends. Often these non-Communists feel persuaded to echo the *Daily Worker* in effect through fear that wide revelations of the extent of the conspiracy's influence will affect individuals whom they know or the camp to which they belong.

Former Secretary of the Interior Harold L. Ickes was in the front line of these attackers. His caustic comments on the ex-Reds who help the government paralleled his almost unrestricted praise of Soviet Russia in World War II. Writing in the *New Republic* of May 1, 1950, in connection with the Tydings Committee hearings on Owen Lattimore, he described me as "a creature of a lower order." Not content with that, Ickes added: "He has adopted a new avocation—that of jumping into any convenient witness box to charge decent citizens, on hearsay, with being Communists." Apparently the former Secretary of the Interior was not affected by the rebuttal which came from Judge Learned Hand, in his opinion on the trial of the eleven Communist leaders in the Circuit Court of Appeals. Justice Hand, who has certainly enjoyed a long reputation as a liberal, declared me "well-qualified as an expert" on the Red conspiracy. Despite that characterization, Ickes returned time and again to the charge, thereby aiding the Reds. In the *New Republic* of October 1, 1951, Ickes attacked what the *Daily Worker* termed, in praising him, as "Budenz-Bentley careerism." He merited the Reds' approval, by opposing the conviction of the eleven Communist leaders at Foley Square. Of that conviction Ickes wrote:

Even the Supreme Court, as was shown by its regrettable decision in the case of the eleven Communists, with only Justices Black and Douglas dissenting, has apparently been affected by the thought-terrorists and their supporting claque of professional former Communists under the leadership of such undesirable persons as Budenz and Bentley.

No warmer apology for the "right" of Stalin's agents to undermine the United States government has been penned.

It is amazing, but likewise illustrative, that one of our delegates to the United Nations, Mrs. Eleanor Roosevelt, has joined this chorus. In her syndicated column, appearing in the New York *World-Telegram,* on August 16, 1948, Mrs. Roosevelt rushed to the defense of Alger Hiss, whose case was then being considered by the House Committee on Un-American Activities. Admitting that "there certainly were efforts at Communist espionage in this country during the war," Mrs. Roosevelt said: "Yet I disapprove very much of the way in which these legislative committees work. Smearing good people like Lauchlin Currie, Alger Hiss, and others is, I think, unforgivable. . . . Anyone knowing either Mr. Currie or Mr. Hiss, who are the two I happen to know fairly well, would not need any denial on their part to know they are not Communists."

Such observations were preparatory to reflecting upon the character and credibility of Whittaker Chambers, in the midst of the first trial of Alger Hiss. On June 8, 1949, Mrs. Roosevelt issued a column under the heading: "Who IS On Trial—Chambers or Hiss?" At a moment when Chambers was the victim of a whispering campaign of the filthiest kind, Mrs. Roosevelt wrote: "Day by day, as the defense attorney in the perjury trial of Alger Hiss, former State Department official, brings out facts about Whittaker Chambers as a witness, one cannot help being mystified as to why the gentleman should be believed at all. . . . He seems to have no hesitation about telling various unsavory facts about his private life, which makes him seem less and less valuable as a witness. One gets the feeling as one reads the newspaper accounts that Mr. Chambers is on trial and not Mr. Hiss."

Counsel for Hiss, as is always the rule in such cases, did try to put Chambers on trial, and Mrs. Roosevelt's words, so widely disseminated, only aided these lawyers in that effort.

When the evidence was so overwhelming in the second trial of Alger Hiss that he was convicted, Mrs. Roosevelt made no apology to Chambers. Nor did she commend him for his services to American security or express regret for the indignities he had suffered. Her sadness was all for Stalin's agent who had damaged the United States so seriously. On that score she said: "It is a very difficult case to know what to think. I never once heard him [Hiss] say anything that would even approve the idea that he was a Communist. I feel that he may have perjured himself, but I don't feel he ever sold any secret papers. It's a very sad case."

There had been no allegation that Hiss had "sold" secret documents; the accusation was that as a loyal member of the notorious Ware cell in Washington, he had obtained papers for Stalin. Moreover, it was well known that as one of President Roosevelt's chief advisers at Yalta he had worked for the betrayal of Poland and the serious weakening of Nationalist China.

It must be added that during Hiss's second trial Mrs. Roosevelt again assailed Chambers as an incredible witness. And the same treatment was meted out by her to Elizabeth Bentley. On August 4, 1948, in a column entitled: "Spy Queen's Story," Mrs. Roosevelt characterized Miss Bentley's testimony as "the fantastic story of this evidently neurotic lady." Mrs. Roosevelt was particularly warm in her defense of Lauchlin Currie, executive assistant to the late President, who, Miss Bentley states, had furnished confidential information to her. Since then, Mr. Currie has been named, in testimony under oath before the McCarran Subcommittee, as an active participant in the famous conference in 1942 between Earl Browder and Robert Minor, Communist leaders, on the one hand, and Sumner Welles, Under Secretary of State, on the other. That conference, we know, was openly asserted by Browder to have affected the whole American policy toward the Communists in China.

Continuing her excoriation of Miss Bentley, Mrs. Roosevelt wrote: "In the future, I should think it might be difficult for her to find any acquaintances who would be willing to say 'Good morning' and 'Good evening' to her. That might be construed as a means to involve them in some new and fantastic trial."

This invitation for the social ostracism of Miss Bentley was consistently pursued as late as August 15, 1951, with a column headed "Many Ex-Reds Testify Only To Save

Their Skins." That was a drastically inaccurate statement, since only those ex-Communists who slip out of the party inconspicuously and refuse to co-operate with the government are allowed to live in peace. They are never publicly criticized for their failure to make amends for their past Red crimes by helping to save America. Nor are they inconvenienced in any way.

In this column, Mrs. Roosevelt said in part: "From my point of view, though I recognize the value to the FBI of information given by ex-Communists, I cannot trust either the motives or sincerity of the ex-Communists who give that information." She then goes on to repeat that they testify in order "to save their own skins." To that she adds: "It is wonderful what good memories many of them have today." If this were true, it cannot be seen what value any information from an ex-Communist would be to the Federal Bureau of Investigation, for it implies that they are engaged in the "lying fantasies" to which the *Daily Worker* refers. It would also imply that the Communist conspiracy should be left untouched, since the government apparently finds it cannot proceed against the conspirators without the testimony of the ex-Communists. That is precisely what Mrs. Roosevelt would do away with, for while she states that she would allow ex-Reds to earn a living, she would deny them "the limelight and sense of importance" that comes from testifying. If there is anything that ex-Communists wish, it is to remain out of any "limelight" and to be relieved of all obligation to testify.

In contrast to these attacks on ex-Communists who served the government, which have included special references to me, has been Mrs. Roosevelt's defense of the Soviet espionage agent, Agnes Smedley. When General Willoughby, Chief Intelligence Officer for General Mac-

Arthur, named Miss Smedley as a member of the Richard Sorge spy ring, she threatened to sue General MacArthur for libel if he would waive his official position. It was General Willoughby, not General MacArthur, who was directly involved, and he offered to make such a waiver, but Miss Smedley never acted. She just got the publicity of the libel threat. Mrs. Roosevelt immediately applauded her for telling off "the brass hats" in the army. Since that time Miss Smedley has died, leaving her ashes to the Red revolutionary cemetery at Peiping, where the faithful Soviet agents in China are buried, and her money to Chu-teh, head of the Chinese Red military forces.

When the cases of Alger Hiss and William W. Remington first became public, Mrs. Roosevelt came to the aid of both by implication when she deplored the fact that: "If a young man [in the government service] had been afflicted with liberal tendencies or had been foolish enough to belong to one or two radical organizations in youth, then he must expect to lose his job and find many other jobs closed to him."

Mrs. Roosevelt's shafts at the ex-Communists who co-operate with government agencies are all the more striking in that she has tempered her advocacy of Soviet-American friendship recently with condemnation of Soviet Russia as "a police state." It is historically a matter of record that this police state has had a consistent policy in regard to ex-Reds throughout the world. It has pursued them to the point of gangster-like crime, notably in the cases of Ignaz Maria Reiss and Juliet Stuart Poyntz. Character assassination has also been the standard Soviet weapon, filling the pages of official Red directive organs in every country.

During the Chambers-Hiss episode, certain newspapers,

in contrast to their caustic attitude toward Chambers, expressed a sadness amounting to sympathy for Hiss. The *Washington Post,* whose news sections often differ from its editorial page, stated editorially: "Hiss had the misfortune of being tempted to betray his country in an era of widespread illusions about Communism and of being tried for perjury . . . in a period of cold war when the pendulum of public sentiment had swung far in the other direction.

"It is difficult to believe that a man of Hiss' training and reputation could commit a similar offense in the climate of today's international politics."

This was written down for public consumption even though Hiss had shown no change of heart and no disposition to aid the government in exposing his confederates.

Such an influential paper as the New York *Times* took so sorrowful a tone in its editorial, "Mr. Hiss Found Guilty," that it provoked the following comment from Steen M. Johnson in the "Letters to the Editor" column: "Is the nation mourning the conviction of Alger Hiss? One would think so from your editorial. Isn't there a deeper meaning to the American people than a feeling of 'pathos and tragedy' for Mr. Hiss?" [2]

The smear of the ex-Reds who appear on the witness stand under subpoena reached a new climax in 1951, centering around the Wallace-Alsop assertions. On October 1 of that year, the *Daily Worker,* directive-giver for the conspiracy, called for a new barrage of vilification against those ex-Communists who testified for the government. This was followed up a few weeks later with more exten-

[2] Critical reference to the *Washington Post* editorial and the New York *Times* statement appeared in the column by Westbrook Pegler, New York *Journal American,* January 28, 1950.

sive directives in the *Daily Worker*. It was made a major
Red objective in *Political Affairs* for October 1951.

According to the *Daily Worker* of October 1, the campaign was to be directed against three in particular:
Whittaker Chambers, Elizabeth Bentley, and me. The
"well-paid, lying fantasies" of this trio of "stool pigeons,"
to use the choice language of the Red paper, were to be
ruthlessly assailed.

We may well inquire how it happened that this new
enterprise in vituperation was inaugurated. The *Daily
Worker* admitted, in effect, that it was encouraged by the
attacks upon me by Joseph Alsop, a syndicated columnist
connected with the New York *Herald Tribune,* and upon
the trio by former Secretary of the Interior Harold Ickes.
The latter frankly let it be known, as we have seen, that
his interest was in obtaining the freedom of the eleven
Communist leaders convicted before Judge Harold Medina at Foley Square. That also gives a partial inkling of
the Red objective.

As for Mr. Alsop, his case deserves examination, since
the Communists made extensive use of his utterances.
They spread his "charges" into many parts of the nation
for the benefit of their cause. Alsop began by accusing
me in his column of contradicting before the McCarran
Subcommittee my previous testimony before the Tydings
Committee in 1950 on John Stewart Service and John
Carter Vincent. It is interesting to note that Mr. Service
was detected by the Federal Bureau of Investigation in
the *Amerasia* case of having given confidential documents
to Philip Jaffe, now identified by testimony as a Soviet
espionage agent. Service did admit that he had been
"an errand boy" for Jaffe, and was recently dismissed
from his post after his eighth hearing on charges of disloyalty. According to the sworn testimony of Admiral

Charles Maynard Cook, Mr. Vincent, who succeeded an anti-Communist, Eugene Dooman, as head of the Far Eastern Division of the State Department, advised the United States government to destroy our war matériel in the Pacific rather than hand it over to Chiang Kai-shek. Both Vincent and Service were commended by the *Daily Worker* in 1945 for having brought about the resignation of General Patrick Hurley as Ambassador to China.

What Mr. Alsop said in defense of these men about my testimony is manifestly incorrect. There was no contradiction between what I told the McCarran and Tydings investigating committees. That was proved definitely at my second appearance before the McCarran Committee. In regard to Service, I had stated in both instances that he had been referred to among the members of the Communist high command as "Lattimore's pupil"—a political phrase—but that I could not recall his ever having been mentioned definitely as a member of the Communist Party. When asked about Mr. Vincent, and some others, in the executive session of the Tydings Committee, I had requested permission to include their names and descriptions of what I knew of them in a list which I had agreed to furnish the committee. This request was granted, Senator Bourke Hickenlooper of Iowa stating that he would not press the questions at that time. Subsequently I wrote the Tydings Committee stating that I would have the list ready by September, 1950, but the committee saw fit to end its activities before that time. The allegation of Mr. Alsop that I was pressed to answer on Mr. Vincent and refused to do so was therefore inaccurate.

The columnist then concentrated on a most extraordinary effort—an attempt to prove that the recommendations made by former Vice President Henry A. Wallace on his famous trip to Soviet Asia and China in 1944 were anti-Communist. Alsop based his assertion on the fact that a telegram sent by Wallace from Kunming in China, released by the former Vice President only seven years later, had recommended that General Joseph Stilwell be superseded in the China area of his Far Eastern command by Lieutenant General Albert E. Wedemeyer. The columnist terms that "an anti-Communist act." He alleges that the revelation of this act reflects upon my credibility, since I had testified that the Communists were confident that Wallace would be of help to them in his China-Soviet Asia mission and indicated their pleasure at that undertaking.

Now, what actually came of the Wallace mission? These things, among others, may be cited. First of all, Mr. Wallace praised the Kolyma gold-mining slave-labor empire in northeastern Siberia, both at a speech in Irkutsk in Soviet Siberia during the course of the trip and in his book, *Soviet Asia Mission*. (That work, incidentally, was ghost-written by A. J. Steiger, a writer on Marxist subjects, identified under oath as a Communist.) The Wallace commendatory representation of the gold-mining slave-labor empire has been demolished by Elinor Lipper [3] who was a prisoner in the very camp Mr. Wallace visited at the time he was there. Incidentally, Mr. Wallace was only repeating in his book what his traveling companion, Owen Lattimore, had stated in the *National Geographic Magazine* for December, 1944.

Second, in his first address after returning home in the summer of 1944, Mr. Wallace declared in effect that Nationalist China would receive aid from the United States only if it established "Soviet-Chinese friendship" and "ended the civil war in China." Although Mr. Wallace may not have been aware of it, the latter phrase was a

[3] *Eleven Years in Soviet Prison Camps*, Henry Regnery Company, 1951.

Communist slogan, which the Reds used for the purpose of winning freedom of movement for the Chinese Communists to operate over the whole country. For this statement the then Vice President was hailed as "a great statesman" by the *Daily Worker*.

Third, in the midst of his trip to Asia, Mr. Wallace sanctioned the use of his name as the author of a pamphlet actually written by Mrs. Owen Lattimore, *Our Job in the Pacific*. It was issued by the Institute of Pacific Relations, and was so pleasing to the Communists that Frederick Vanderbilt Field commended it in the *Daily Worker* and placed it beside Earl Browder's booklet on Teheran. It was an unprecedented act in Red circles to compare favorably the reputed work of a non-Communist with that of a Communist leader, particularly one who was then being hailed as "the leading Marxist-Leninist in the Western Hemisphere."

Fourth, in the Wallace wire from China, which was not made public for seven years, the former Vice President represented Chiang Kai-shek as befuddled, bewildered, and generally unable to cope with the situation. That is the manner in which the Reds were picturing the Chinese Nationalist leader at that time. They even expressed solicitude that in his weakness he might be the victim of a "coup" from certain elements in the Kuomintang. The Reds wanted him represented in this fashion, as any careful reading of the *Daily Worker* for 1944 and 1945 will show, to pave the way for their urgent demand for "coalition government" and to get American acceptance of that proposal. This demand was not formally made of the "allies" until January 1, 1945, when Mao Tse-tung demanded "a government of unity" in China.

Fifth, as for General Stilwell, by 1944 the Communists were no longer interested in his retention of any authority in the Chinese area, as he had outlived his usefulness to them. He was not a Communist, but merely one whom they had worked upon for their own purposes. Their indifference to his fate in 1944 is shown by the fact that they made no fight for him and by the further fact that Frederick Vanderbilt Field in the *Daily Worker* at that time spoke well of General Wedemeyer and indicated that Stilwell's departure had been no loss. The Reds misjudged Wedemeyer, thinking him to be of a school of thought that would agree with them in China. They began to attack him only in 1945, when they discovered that he would not be their tool and after the so-called cold war was assured. Examination of Communist documents, and particularly of the *Daily Worker* for 1944, will prove that the Reds had little interest in American personnel in China during that year but had concentrated on planting in the American mind the idea that Chiang Kai-shek was a weakling and was befuddled.

The Communists felt so warm toward Mr. Wallace after his Asiatic trip that they enthusiastically endorsed him for Vice President—especially after Moscow indicated this was its will. In early 1945, the conspiracy conducted an intensive campaign, of which I had in large part charge, to promote the former Vice President for the post of Secretary of Commerce. The pages of the *Daily Worker* during early 1945 ring out in praise of him. When Jacques Duclos, General Secretary of the Communist Party of France, and known as "the voice of Moscow to the West," denounced Earl Browder as a "revisionist" in April 1945, he accompanied this denunciation of the ill-fated Red chief with commendation of Henry A. Wallace. The American Communists were quick to understand this unprecedented reference to a non-Communist in order to deprecate the views and work of a Red leader.

They hastened to make Wallace their "mass leader" in the political field, when they ran him for the presidency on the Progressive Party ticket.

With this record, and remembering Mr. Wallace's unmitigated praise of Soviet Russia in 1942 and 1943, the picturing of him as engaged in extensive anti-Communist acts strains the credulity of the normal American. But when Mr. Alsop admits before the McCarran Subcommittee that the main point of issue—the political status of one of Mr. Wallace's chief companions on the Asiatic trip, John Carter Vincent—is unknown to him, the irresponsible character of his attacks becomes more evident. For he has hurled the word "perjury" about with some abandon in his assault on my testimony, as the above review of the facts sustains. That the Reds would use his words to aid their conspiracy was a foregone conclusion.

This is underlined by the Alsop statement that I am "almost a professional informer." This is what the *Daily Worker* has been saying for the past five years; that is its precise language, many times repeated. It was echoed first by Owen Lattimore before the Tydings Committee in the spring of 1950 when he termed me "an overworked informer." The animus in such phrases can easily be seen. The President of the United States has asked publicly that all citizens co-operate with the Federal Bureau of Investigation. That I have given three thousand hours of my time without remuneration during the past five years to the FBI becomes "professional informing" in the utterances of Alsop, Lattimore, and the Communist press. That I testified under subpoena and against my inclination at the trial of the eleven Communist leaders at Foley Square, having been kept on the witness stand for two weeks, is according to these sources, in the same category.

That, under court orders, I testified against such under-cover leaders of the conspiracy as Gerhart Eisler, J. Peters, and John Santo with decisions against them in all cases, is likewise considered an unworthy act.

This concept is grist for the Communist mills and provides one of the greatest aids to the conspiracy. When Senator Herbert H. Lehman of New York suggested that there be a special investigation by the Senate of Alsop's "charges"—although there was a responsible committee headed by Senator Pat McCarran and composed of former judges and attorney generals already investigating subversion—the *Daily Worker* gave front-page headlines to Lehman's declarations. Indeed, the Red paper reprinted the account two days in succession, running the Senator's picture prominently on each occasion. This though in the professed Communist view, Mr. Lehman is all the wrong things—a millionaire several times over, an investment banker, and an important member of that "Wall Street oligarchy" which the Communists attack. In addition, the Reds issued an official declaration of their national committee in the October 1951 issue of *Political Affairs,* demanding the release of the eleven Red leaders convicted at Foley Square. One reason given was this: "The present Washington exposures of stool pigeon Budenz, who was the star witness for the government at Foley Square against the Communist leaders, will soon show him to all as unworthy of any credence." It does not bother the Reds that there were no "exposures" but, as we have seen, merely distortions of testimony and the facts by men like Alsop into fictions or fictitious interpretations of events helpful to the conspiracy.

Not deterred by the Communist praise of his efforts, Alsop rehashed all his previous statements in an article in the *Atlantic Monthly* for April, 1952. Nowhere does

he acknowledge there that my testimony as to Owen Lattimore's affinity for the Chinese Communists has been
confirmed by numerous witnesses, including former Governor Harold E. Stassen of Minnesota and former Ambassador to Soviet Russia, William C. Bullitt. Nor does
he choose to recognize that John Carter Vincent's own
testimony before the McCarran Committee was of such
a character that *Time* magazine stated it had shown Vincent to be one of the architects of the tragic American
policy which led to Communist victory in China.

Alsop's reference to my "belated recollection" is ridic-
ulous. No ex-Communist rushes out to testify unless he
is subpoenaed and asked directly about specific subjects.
I have insisted from the very beginning that I would not
testify except under such subpoena and upon matters
directly asked of me. This is the orderly and proper way
in which to act. When I am questioned under oath, by
order of court or committee, as to matters with which I
became familiar as a leading Communist, I am obliged to
tell the truth, no matter what learned persons may be
involved and what personal inconvenience I am put to.
What Alsop's attacks amount to is a demand that I either
defy subpoenas or perjure myself.

There is no one who contends that the testimony of an
ex-Communist, particularly in regard to individuals, does
not require corroboration, either by official Communist
documents or by witnesses. No ex-Communist has ever
made such a contention. The striking thing is that such
testimony has been corroborated in a degree which it
might be well to have in all cases before our courts. It is
precisely because it has been corroborated to such a degree by documents or by witnesses who could not have
any conection with each other that it has so stridently
aroused the outcries of the Reds and their allies.

The damaging effect of the assault upon the ex-Reds who testify for the government is that the number of such witnesses is diminishing. As a result, the American nation is permitting itself to be disarmed at home in a most serious manner. As Senator Pat McCarran declared in an interview in the *United States News and World Report* of November 16, 1951:

Of course, the obvious fact is that often the only way you can get direct evidence about a conspiracy is from a witness who was one of the conspirators. If the Communists can succeed in discrediting all former Communists in the public mind, they protect themselves and wreak vengeance on those who may have turned against the conspiracy, and, at the same time, set up a deterrent against any Communist's breaking with the party. There is nothing the Communists would like better than to make it true that "once a Communist always a Communist." That would simplify things for the Communist Party.

The tragic reality is that so many American statesmen, who do not or will not take the trouble to examine Communist documents will lend themselves at least indirectly to this assistance to Stalin's conspiracy. It is equally regrettable that a number of editors of responsible newspapers, some of them ill-informed on the Communist line, will open their pages to such smears, originated by the Kremlin's agents.

That is one other outstanding explanation of why the United States has been so severely defeated by Soviet aggression. The conspiracy has been enabled to continue effectively its work of subversion and confusion within this country, and out of it all has come the vacillation which has spelled American retreat.

# CHAPTER 7

# Stalin's Entry into Education

When Stalin started planning World War III, directed primarily against the United States, he quite naturally sought the aid and encouragement of certain leading educators. With them he associated generous-hearted benefactors of research projects dedicated to forward higher education. The result was the World Congress of Intellectuals of 1949, which raised the curtain on nothing more than Stalin's determination to destroy the morale of non-Soviet nations.

Already in 1924, in lectures delivered at the Sverdlov University in Moscow, Stalin had specified "cultural and educational organizations" as valuable allies in the Communist struggle for world dictatorship.[1] These were to be groups initiated by the Communists or infiltrated and captured by them. From the early thirties onward the Soviet fifth column in this country obediently courted America's free-minded young educators. The powerful weapon that these men and women would wield in the

[1] These Stalin lectures are the now famous *Foundations of Leninism,* published and studied on such a widespread scale by the Communists.

arena of public opinion was obvious to the conspirators.

While the average American imagines that he identifies the educator only with the classroom, he does not realize the weight he gives to opinions by a "professor" on almost any subject. If a physics instructor expresses political views, he is harkened to as a sort of latter-day prophet. The Communists understand clearly this universal respect for "learning." They go so far as to draw from parent-teacher associations, civic groups, and the community-at-large. Not the least of Stalin's successes in converting America's victory in World War II into a bewildered postwar retreat has been the work of Communist-led "intellectuals."

Much has been written about Soviet psychological warfare in other countries. Actually the most decisive features of this psychological warfare have been carried on in the U.S.A. It was the recognition of this influence which led V. J. Jerome, one of the two top men in the Communist cultural commission, to praise those American educators and other professional representatives who had stood with the Communist conspiracy in its aid to Hitler during "the second imperialist war." The year was 1940, and Mr. Jerome was hard-pressed. Endeavoring to instruct intellectuals, he declared: "The moment has come for unequivocating choice, to take a clear-cut position—with the common people for peace and socialism, or in the camp of imperialism for war and reaction." How reminiscent are those phrases of what the Soviet fifth column says today, in even more strident tones. Jerome proclaimed this the "great test," and added proudly: "Most intellectuals who have been attracted to the working-class cause, to the Soviet peace policy, to Communism, stood the test, and stood it well." He paid tribute to the "hundreds of decent, modest intellectuals who stand guard at their posts despite reaction's offensive." Well might he praise them, for these Reds and their friends had served as an effective cover for the big strikes against American production, engineered by the Communists at Allis-Chalmers and the North American Aircraft Corporation during the period of the Hitler-Stalin Pact. They had also served as defenders of Communist front organizations. They struck blows at American security production as serious as those the Soviet agents actually did out in the field.[2]

It was also the recognition of how the educator can influence the community that caused the *Daily Worker* on October 25, 1944, to declare approvingly that "teachers are graduating into the school of life." It commended the "schoolmarms" who were getting out into the streets and neighborhoods and organizing the people. It mentioned specifically "such personalities as Dr. Bella V. Dodd,[3] now vice president of the Communist Political Association, who half a dozen years ago was still the most popular teacher in Hunter College; or Doxey Wilkerson, who left Howard University . . . to become the executive editor of that great newspaper, the *People's Voice*." [Communist newspaper published in Los Angeles.] And the *Daily Worker* proceeded to point out as further examples "the heroic figures of Professors Langevin and Joliot-Curie" in France; the latter had just announced that he and his wife were Communists. That Joliot-Curie's position was of value to the Kremlin can be understood when we recall that for a number of years he was head of the French Atomic Energy Commission, during which time he made several trips to Moscow to consult Stalin,

[2] The comments by V. J. Jerome appear in his pamphlet, *The Intellectuals and the War*.

[3] Dr. Bella Dodd left the Communist Party in 1949 and in 1952 indicated direct opposition to the party.

as well as trips to the United States to consult some of our foremost atomic scientists.

At this time, in 1944, the Communists in the United States were ostensibly supporting the Roosevelt Administration for their own purposes, which were, specifically, to advance their own infiltration in certain important and influential groups. Accordingly, the *Daily Worker* extolled the formation of the National Educators for Roosevelt Committee and pointed out significantly that among its members were such veteran Communist fronters as Albert Einstein of Princeton University, Thomas Mann, the German author, also a lecturer at Princeton, and W. E. B. DuBois, the well-known Negro educator. Subsequent events were to show that the work of these men for Roosevelt was to lay the foundation for their service on Communist "peace" fronts in the 1945–51 period.

The Progressive Party movement in support of Henry A. Wallace for President in 1948 had as its backbone such members of college faculties as Professor Thomas I. Emerson of the Yale University Law School. The party could not have had the effectiveness it did without the substantial support of the professors. The vote that the Progressive Party received did not come up to Communist predictions nor to the pre-election broadcasts of the Moscow radio. But it did serve as an intimidating force over certain politicians, just as the Communist-dominated American Labor Party has affected the political atmosphere of New York State and led to strong appeasement in high political circles there.

The indirect as well as direct effect of pro-Communist educators in at least creating uncertainty in the American mind and among American officialdom was evident in the personnel of the very first front organizations. Among these were the Congress of American Revolutionary Writers, the various student movements, and the American League Against War and Fascism. In immediate prominence as founders were such men as Dr. Robert Morss Lovett of the University of Chicago and Dr. Harry F. Ward of Union Theological Seminary, whose ability to reach those in high public positions we have previously observed. In addition, there were others such as the late Genevieve Taggard, professor at Sarah Lawrence College in Bronxville, New York, some of whose faculty members have made a marked contribution to these causes, and Professor Frederick L. Schuman of Williams College. Associated with them was Professor H. W. L. Dana, contributor to *Soviet Russia Today* and *New Masses,* who carried the prestige of being the grandson of Henry Wadsworth Longfellow.

The parade of men and women of such professional standing continues to the present day. Howard Fast, Communist writer, in a eulogy on the Cultural and Scientific Conference for World Peace held in New York City in 1949, wrote:

Without question, the leadership of such men as Harlow Shapley, Olin Downes, Albert Einstein, and Thomas Mann played a very significant part in both the mobilization for the conference and the carrying through of its purpose. Particularly were Shapley and Downes instrumental in the struggle for unity. . . . We must not underestimate the strength of such people, the integrity and consistency of them—and we must understand that they play their role in one of the most difficult periods of our country's history.

In addition, Fast pays tribute to Marshall Dimock, former professor of Northwestern University and consultant to the Department of Defense since 1948, Dr. Allen M. Butler, and, of course, to Lovett, Schuman, Philip Morrison, and Mary Van Kleeck, whose influence in the educational world by virtue of her long-held post at the Russell Sage Foundation is not to be discounted.

One major cause of Communist interest in education and in educators is the effect on the students. The Communists want to get their hands on American youth by every means possible. Lenin's injunctions on the value of young people in the revolutionary struggle to destroy the non-Soviet states are in force today. They are particularly useful now in the present Soviet attack on "American imperialism." It is vital for the success of the Communist conspiracy to break down the morale of the young men drafted for military service and to lay the foundations for sedition or defeatism among them. Thus, Earl Browder, during the Hitler-Stalin alliance, warned that the "Wall Street war program is the inexorable foe of everything progressive in the educational field."

The important point is not so much where the Communists and their sympathizers stand on a particular issue, but the basic reason for their position. The Communists, for example, have been successively anti-Hitler, pro-Hitler, and then again anti-Hitler. During the period of the Hitler-Stalin Pact they violently opposed American intervention and castigated Roosevelt for aiding the Allies; the late President later, of course, became their alleged hero. At one time the Communist-dominated labor unions did their utmost to impede war production; during the war no unions were more co-operative with management than these. Because the Communists opposed intervention in the war until Hitler's declaration of war on Russia, or because they now oppose universal military training does not in itself make these positions wrong, nor should it add any lustre to the moral standing of the pro-Communists. The important fact is that these positions, like all others of the Communists, are dictated by Moscow and have only one purpose—to serve the ultimate ends of the Soviet conspiracy: world revolution and the world Soviet dictatorship.

It was also during the Hitler-Stalin liaison that Dr. Margaret Schlauch, Professor of English at New York University, took the lead in organizing large groups of students in the Communist May Day parade of 1941, which was dedicated to all-out aid to Hitler. Through her advice and work among faculty members of various colleges, sizable delegations of the American Student Union from the City College of New York, Brooklyn College, Hunter College, Queens College, New York University, Sarah Lawrence College, Columbia University, and Barnard College were prominent in the parade. This was the time of the Rapp-Coudert Committee's inquiry into subversion in the public schools and public institutions of higher learning of New York State. These delegations made the inquiry a major issue, chanting as they marched: "Stop the Rapp Investigation!" But their slogans and acts were also directed against "the imperialist war." Margaret Schlauch crowned her subversive career, which included membership in fifty Communist fronts, by relinquishing her post to teach in the schools of Stalin's Poland. She is no doubt doing well in her present post of indoctrinating Poland's youth with Communism—she had years of practice in the classrooms of New York University on Washington Square.

One must not underestimate the results of these student demonstrations. Encouraged by Red educators and supported by statements of the American Peace Mobilization and other subversive fronts, they injured American morale and slowed down defense preparations. They were at a high peak of effectiveness when the invasion of Soviet Russia by Hitler ended them.

How reminiscent the statements and acts of the Hitler-Stalin Pact period are to those issued by the Communists today can be readily seen from the proceedings of the Fifteenth National Convention of the Communist Party. In its directives "youth in the fight for peace and against militarization" is given an outstanding position. The following aims are stipulated: "No militarization of the schools and classrooms. Defend academic freedom. Defend student deferments." How familiar are the words which ring out in the claim that "the sum and substance of the imperialists' aim is a whole generation of youth harnessed to their war machine." The Communists were not concerned, from Hitler's attack on Russia to the end of the war, about militarization or the harnessing of youth to the war machine.

We get a good glimpse of what "no militarization of the schools and classrooms" means when we read further: "Ways can be found to give voice to the public indignation at the war hysteria and chauvinism being injected into the schools and communities, especially in the guise of atom bomb drills and civilian defense mobilization." It is quite obvious in this and other statements what the Reds are after: to leave our civilian defense completely unprepared and our school children at the mercy of any invaders. That is in line with the instruction to emphasize that "the draft and universal military service and training proposals are highly unwelcome" and to accentuate among college students that they should not cut short their studies for military service. Such propaganda is not based on true opposition to war, but is simply a part of the Soviet offensive against the United States, the purpose of which is to make our youth both spiritually and intellectually unprepared for American defense.[3]

The participation of college professors in mass meetings and demonstrations at which the United States is denounced as "imperialist" and "warmongering" advances these views among the students. Among the Americans who attended the World Congress of Intellectuals in 1949, Stalin's opening gun against the United States, was Colston E. Warne, member of the faculty of small and conservative Amherst College, the alma mater of Calvin Coolidge. Although a member of thirty Communist fronts and a leading figure in the Consumers Union, which the Communists have used to penetrate other groups, Warne was a consultant for the President's Economic Advisory Council. He has also remained for twenty years on Amherst's staff. This professor rose at the conference in the Waldorf-Astoria of 1949 to criticize bitterly the rearmament program as leading America to a war economy. Even though Warne has defended the Communist Party in the past, and continued to be prominent in forwarding Soviet causes, nevertheless he was undisturbed in his official connections with the government.

Social work is a field in which the Communists have exercised considerable influence. An example is Professor Marion Hathway, who has taken a consistently pro-Soviet stand. Although affiliated with at least forty Communist fronts, she retained her position in the de-

---

[3] The edited proceedings of the *Fifteenth National Convention of the Communist Party,* held in December, 1950, are published in *Political Affairs* of February, 1951.

partment of social work at the supposedly conservative University of Pittsburgh for almost twenty years and left there only last August to head one of the graduate departments at Bryn Mawr College. Her long devotion to the movements which aid Stalin is indicated in her sponsorship of the Spanish Rescue Ship Mission of 1941, devised to bring such professional agents of Moscow as Gerhardt Eisler and Paul Merker to this country. We must remember that this group was transformed later into the Joint Anti-Fascist Refugee Committee, which, under the direction of Robert William Weiner, head of the conspiratorial funds of the Communist International apparatus, smuggled many leading Reds into the Western Hemisphere. Professor Hathway's latest contribution to Communism was her membership in the Scientific and Cultural Conference for World Peace, a Moscow-inspired creation to forward the war against the United States.

Another sponsor of twenty Communist fronts who has been in a position to influence the thinking of students is Dorothy Brewster, professor of English at Columbia University. She entered the arena early by defending the 1936-38 purges in Soviet Russia, by assailing the findings of the John Dewey Committee in regard to Leon Trotsky, and by working hard in the American Writers Congress, even during the Hitler-Stalin Pact era. Quite naturally, she has participated in the recent denunciations of the "war aims" of the United States. Alongside her can be placed Dorothy W. Douglas of Smith College, member of a comparable number of fronts. This instructor in a college that develops many leaders has likewise asserted that Stalin's regime has done much good for the Russian people, has defended the purges as necessary "protection" for the dictatorship, and has recently been a sponsor of the Cominform-touted Stockholm Peace Petition.

Another promotor of the Stockholm "petition" is Dr. Allen M. Butler, faculty member of the Harvard University Medical School, who is affiliated with ten fronts. Almost a dean among those sponsoring Communist-dominated groups was the late Walter Rautenstrauch, professor emeritus of Industrial Engineering at Columbia University, whose prestige was of aid to fifty such organizations. Also from Columbia University aid to the Communist "peace fronts" has been given by Dr. Theodor Rosebury, bacteriologist, Professors Michael Heidelberger, Robert S. Lynd, Bernhard J. Stern, and Dr. Goodwin Watson of Teachers College. The Institute for Advanced Studies at Princeton University is ably represented on Communist front by Professor Erwin Panofsky. New York University has contributed, in addition to Margaret Schlauch, Eda Lou Walton, Lyman K. Bradley (who went to jail for his pro-Communist activities), and Henry Pratt Fairchild, among others.

· Dr. Fairchild is an excellent example of the influence on higher learning of pro-Soviet education. Hundreds of students have been influenced by him. Among them are young men whose loyalty we must count on in our fighting forces. With his long record of membership in forty fronts, it is not surprising that he was among the first to arrange for American support for the so-called World Peace Congress of 1949, organized by such Soviet agents as Boleslaw K. Gebert, whose record of subversion runs from his activities in Chicago and Detroit as an illegal alien to his present assignment for the Soviet-ruled World Federation of Trade Unions to wreck the economy of the democratic countries. Gebert was a big figure also in the International Workers Order, the insurance adjunct of the Communist conspiracy in this country.

One of the conspicuous pro-Communist acts of Dr. Fairchild was his leadership in the committee which attacked the Federal Bureau of Investigation in 1940. At that time the Communists were doing everything in their power to prevent defense production in this country and Britain, and were planning "to turn the imperialist war into civil war" on behalf of Hitler. The FBI had arrested a number of members of the Abraham Lincoln Brigade, the American Communist group that had fought in Spain under Stalin's banner. But the committee of university professors, in which Fairchild played a major part, denounced the FBI for seeking to "spread hysteria and terror" and threw over this sedition the protecting mantle of "constitutional rights." What is more to the point, they were successful. Their success is a measure of what they can do in official quarters today.

These professors, of whom we have only begun to call the roll, affect not only the students of the immediate moment but the community members and leaders of tomorrow. When Dr. Philip Morrison of Cornell University led a delegation of his students to Washington in early 1951, in the seditious "American Peace Crusade," America was warned of what these pro-Communist instructors are up to. But the Women's Club of Scarsdale, New York, later that year gave a demonstration of the more effective influence of the Communist fronts in education. This club, composed of comfortably situated and well-to-do-women, protested the appearance of Rabbi Benjamin Schultz, well-known anti-Communist, before the New York State Federation of Women's Clubs meeting at Elmira. It was known that Rabbi Schultz would review the dangers of Red infiltration into the schools and textbooks of New York State, and the Scarsdale club raised the old banner of "academic freedom" and "constitutional rights." But it went further by reflecting upon Rabbi Schultz' standing in the Jewish community. This was an indirect libel on the Jewish people, projecting the false implication that they are overwhelmingly opposed to any real curb upon Communism and allied influences.

Fortunately, in this case the strategy was not successful. Although a huge smear campaign was started against Rabbi Schultz, who has sacrificed a great deal for his principles, the State Federation voted 114 to 44 in support of a thorough-going investigation into Communist-minded infiltration in the schools and textbooks. But it is significant that a club located in such ultra-suburban surroundings as Scarsdale and composed almost exclusively of college graduates should have taken a stand helpful to the Soviet fifth column.

The Communists and those who work with them have long been interested in the lower schools and have concentrated much effort in that area. The banner-bearer in this field has been the New York Teachers Union, which has consistently followed the party line and has been excluded from both the American Federation of Labor and the Congress of Industrial Organizations on the grounds of Communist control. In 1951 it was also barred on that account from representing the teachers of New York City before the Board of Education. Prominent in the work of this organization have been, in turn, Morris U. Schappes, convicted for perjury in 1941 for swearing that he was not a Communist; Dr. Bella V. Dodd, previously described; and Rose V. Russell, who has staunchly fought for Communist objectives, including the recent "peace" crusades. She was most active in New York City in organizing the Stockholm Peace Petition drive. In 1951, she appeared conspicuously as a representative of eight teachers, tried by a special referee on charges by the superintendent of education that they had refused to state whether or not they were members of the Communist Party. Yet, almost in the midst of these proceedings, Miss Russell received the special award over television for her "contribution" to education. This is a good illustration of how the pro-Red atmosphere created in the radio and television industries, and to which *Red Channels* has called attention, brings prestige to others who labor in the pro-Communist vineyard.

New York City is merely illustrative of the scope and effectiveness of the Communist conspiracy among educators. The same forces are at work throughout the country. In each district of the party organization special means are taken to affect teachers in the grade schools and the high schools. For instance, in Massachusetts, Robenia Anthony, of Local 484, American Federation of Labor, was long ago praised by the *Daily Worker* as a prominent member of the "progressives" in the A.F. of L. She has climaxed membership on a number of fronts through the years by joining the list of sponsors in the call for the National Labor Conference for Peace, engineered in 1949.

As early as 1940, the *Daily Worker* recorded the achievements of those teachers who were working with the Reds in primary and secondary schools. A special article by David Gordon, party name for a teacher in the New York public school system, states: "Teacher-student activity has gone beyond their occupational organizations. Teacher and student are to be found in such organizations as the American League for Peace and Democracy, American Youth Congress, in the progressive political life of the nation. America will never forget the great student peace strikes and demonstrations conducted in our schools in the past several years. Nor will they ever forget the help the teachers gave." The piece ended with directives to "faculty and student" to prevent "Wall Street's ardent war hopes from being foisted on the American people." It ordered that efforts be renewed for "unity" of teacher and pupil in seeking this end.[4]

Such instructions were emphasized again today at the Fifteenth National Convention of the Communist Party, and as an example it cites "the gallant fight of the New York Teacher's Union." Hand in hand with this goes the penetration of parent-teacher associations. On this the Fifteenth Convention said: "There is mounting indignation and protest on the part of parent-teacher associations against militarizing the public schools and terrorizing the minds of children with atom bomb 'defense' drills." In the Communist meaning of words, this is a strict directive to assure that this "indignation" is fostered and forwarded.

Aware of what investigations, particularly initiated by parents, would divulge concerning the Red conspiracy in the schools and colleges, the Communists have raised their old cry of "academic freedom." They urged, at this same convention, "a struggle against Nazi-like control of the mind." In the official proceedings we read denunciations of "the fascist blacklist and censorship campaign," coupled with this exhortation: "An outstanding example

[4] The *Daily Worker,* January 1, 1940, "Lessons Learned After School," by David Gordon.

References to the various names mentioned in this chapter have been taken from the reports of the House Committee on Un-American Activities, and particularly the report previously mentioned in the text, *Communist "Peace" Offensive: A Campaign to Defeat and Disarm the United States,* April, 1951.

of resistance to fascization of the college campus has been
the struggle against the 'loyalty oaths' in California."

Curiously enough, despite our imminent danger, it is
still possible to arouse the feelings of many people by
trumpeting that academic freedom is in jeopardy when
Reds are involved. At the commencement exercises of
Sarah Lawrence College in Bronxville, New York, whose
own faculty has been under investigation by the American Legion, Professor Henry Steele Commager, the historian, spoke up on behalf of "greater intellectual freedom in higher education." According to the New York
*Times* of May 11, 1951, "Professor Commager declared
that education was under attack from Massachusetts to
California, not with Communism as its actual issue but
instead an unwise demand for conformity and censorship
of ideas."

Professor Commager, in 1951, after we have suffered
more than 100,000 casualties in Korea, states to an informed audience that Communism is not "the actual issue." His talk of "censorship" falls completely out of
focus when it is realized that the Communist question in
education is not one of individual views. Every Communist educator or Red sympathizer in education is an
active agent of the conspiracy, whose orders it is his duty
to obey. In his own field, he is just as dangerous as a
Soviet espionage agent.

The Communist educators, like all members of the
Soviet fifth column, cannot merely hold certain opinions; they must act. The fundamental instructions for
all these soldiers in the ranks of Stalin's army were
laid down by William Z. Foster in an article in *The
Communist,* in September, 1938. The very first thing
required of educators, according to Foster, is "a thorough
readiness to accept party discipline." They are also

obliged to receive a thorough "Marxist-Leninist education." They must, in addition, "fight" on behalf of the cause. This makes it necessary, among other things stressed by Foster, that "our teachers must write new school textbooks and rewrite history from the Marxist viewpoint." The professors who are scientists were also ordered to "organize the battle" for spreading Marxist-Leninist ideology among their colleagues. This was stressed more emphatically at the Fifteenth National Convention, when it stated directly that the scientists must take "a clear and consistent stand against the attempt to pervert their knowledge in the service of imperialist destruction." Anyone in the least familiar with Communist directives will understand at once that this is an order to the scientists to halt America's defense preparations by any means.

A few months after Dr. Commager's statement at Sarah Lawrence College, the president of that institution was requested by the Westchester County [New York] American Legion to reply publicly to fourteen questions concerning the faculty and campus activities of the college. These revolved in part around the alleged membership of a prominent member of the faculty on at least five Communist fronts, the sponsorship of the Stalinist Waldorf-Astoria conference in 1949 by another, and the fact that a third had been named by a number of witnesses before the McCarran Senate Subcommittee as an active Communist. There was also involved the question as to whether John Gates, editor of the *Daily Worker,* had not been invited to speak on the campus after his conviction on Foley Square. The board of trustees of the college refused to answer the Legion's questions, stating that the teachers have, under the college's policy, the "right" and "freedom" to belong to any organization they see fit to join.

Nothing shows more clearly how the Red cry of "academic freedom" has succeeded for the Communists than the stand of the National Education Association. This association, which should be in the front line of the fight against seditious influences, has chosen instead to attack those opposing Communist infiltration in our schools. At the San Francisco convention of the NEA in the summer of 1951 several prominent educators charged that those hitting at Communists in educational institutions were actually trying to cut down funds for schools and colleges. An examination of the pages of the *Daily Worker* will reveal that this is the favorite Communist method to obscure the issue. In a letter of July 10, 1951, to the New York *Times,* Otto E. Dohrenwend, chairman of the Citizens Committee in Scarsdale, New York, put a pertinent question to the NEA when he asked: "Why is it that the NEA gets angry at people who expose Communist influences in the schools rather than at the infiltrators who are the real enemies of our public schools?"

His question seems to have produced only more anger, for at the 1951 New York *Herald-Tribune* Forum, Warren Weaver of the Rockefeller Foundation attacked the Citizens Committee in Scarsdale and went so far as to say: "The real issue is whether we shall compromise with an internal totalitarianism which seems to consider itself the only enemy of Communism and which exploits our fear of Communism with evil results to our freedom." Thus, this representative of one of our great foundations which has influence over education, unconsciously echoed the very battle cries of the *Daily Worker*. Perhaps it was this lack of understanding of the Communist conspiracy and its dangers which had led the Rockefeller Foundation in 1940 to vote $20,000 to Hanns Eisler, brother of the Soviet agent Gerhart Eisler, and himself since 1935 head of the Red music bureau in Moscow.

In a letter to the *Herald-Tribune*, published November 14, 1951, Mr. Dohrenwend wrote:

In his forum speech, Mr. Weaver made the absurd charge that we had objected to a dancer because of her "past record of social theory" and to a textbook editor because of his "political tastes." The truth is we objected to these two individuals, as to many others, because of their Red records of affiliation with Communist fronts and causes. Mr. Weaver represented the dancer as performing "in our community," but actually she gave a lecture-dance program in three Scarsdale public schools before student assemblies, including children as young as the third grade. Mr. Weaver did not disclose that we exposed a PTA speaker as a member of the Communist International.

Mr. Weaver's speech concealed the fact that the School Board and the paid staff did act on many of our recommendations; several Howard Fast books are no longer in the library card files; Shirley Graham's book on Paul Robeson was removed as recommended reading; some social studies textbooks have been replaced; certain pamphlets edited by Maxwell Stewart were discontinued.

The personalities mentioned reveal the extent of penetration in the public school system of Scarsdale. It is a good example of what is happening in a number of other communities. The dancer was Pearl Primus, member of a number of Communist fronts and trained in Barney Josephson's Café Society, a New York nightclub organized and frequented by Communists. Her performances were repeatedly played up in the *Daily Worker*. Shirley Graham has been an active Communist-fronter, including support of Gerhart Eisler and a statement on behalf of eleven Communist leaders. Her biography of Paul Robeson was of course eulogistic. Maxwell Stewart, identified as a Communist before the McCarran Subcommittee, has been active in a number of fronts and is the author of an IPR pamphlet in which he pays tribute to the Chinese Communists and represents them as like our Populists.

Several of the books by Howard Fast, open Communist, remain in the library. The Board of Education has permitted the "adult school," which is indirectly connected with the educational system in Scarsdale, to present as a lecturer Dr. Otto Klineberg, associated with a number of Red-sponsored groups.

In addition to the cry for "academic freedom," a plea is made that the effort to rid the schools of Communists is hampering the discussion of ideas and, specifically, any discussion of Communism. This is merely an echo of the *Daily Worker's* constant chant of "thought control," which comes ironically from those who hail the slave state, which is a master in this technique. It is an untrue charge, as Mr. Dohrenwend showed in calling down the Scarsdale school system for its failure to instruct the pupils about Communism on a critical basis and as the proponent of the slave state. That is the attitude of all responsible persons opposing Communist infiltration and influence in the educational system. I myself expressed this view in the *American Legion Magazine* of November 1951:

Communism's theory and practice should be a subject of instruction in the schools, but on the basis of its reality as a slave system, and not on the extravagant fictions brought over here by men like Dr. Philip Morrison of Cornell and Owen Lattimore of Johns Hopkins University. The students should be given a historic knowledge of the Kremlin's plans to achieve world conquest. . . . They should know of the official Red salutations to Stalin as "the leader, teacher, and friend of the peoples of the world" and of the official declarations that Soviet Russia is "the fatherland of the toilers of the world," under which sedition is nurtured in every country.

A few universities do have courses on "The Techniques of Communism," analyzing critically the theory and practice of Communism. These should be more widely adopted as a part of the curriculum. Instead, in too many classrooms Communism is presented "objectively" from the point of view of Soviet Russia and the false allegations of its leaders. Such instruction directly promotes the weakening and eventual destruction of our national security.

A serious feature of the Red conspiracy among educators is the fact that Communist professors and teachers give marked aid to the schools of sedition organized by the Communist Party. There are instructors from a number of universities secretly serving on commissions which have built up the secret training schools of Marxism-Leninism or which have established the more open Red schools such as the Jefferson School of Social Science in New York City. A conspicuous example is Dr. Dirk Struik of the Massachusetts Institute of Technology, who, it is now disclosed, taught in the secret schools for cells in the Boston area. For that and other acts he has now been indicted for conspiracy by a grand jury in Middlesex County, Massachusetts.

Then, too, as a result of secret work for the conspiracy in the colleges, a number of professors have been brought directly into leadership in the Red apparatus. Professor Joseph Cohen of Brooklyn College, now known as Joe Clark, has become a writer for the *Daily Worker* and *New Masses*, and is active in other open Communist work. Dr. Samuel Sillen of the English Department of New York University, a close friend of Margaret Schlauch, was moved over to the *Daily Worker* as editor of the "cultural page." This was done in order that he might also serve as a valuable member of the Communist cultural commission, which directs the infiltration of schools, colleges, the press, radio, and television. He is now editor of *Masses and Mainstream,* Communist magazine for "intellectuals." Dr. Albert Blumberg, who was an honored member of the faculty of Johns Hopkins University a few years ago, left his college post to become district leader for the Communists in Maryland and the District of Columbia. There he was, of course, most active in the direction of infiltration of government departments. Not the least of his advantages in carrying on this underground work was his widespread acquaintance with college faculty members.

The ease with which Communist-front professors operate—Colston Warne and Marshall Dimock are examples—indicates how the penetration of government is achieved directly or indirectly. The equal ease with which big industrialists and other prominent citizens are persuaded to go to the defense of Communists in education illustrates the sad lack of understanding in high circles of Soviet fifth column methods. An outstanding case in point is the committee of prominent people which first went to the rescue of the Communist-fronters in Scarsdale. Among them, for instance, was C. E. Wilson, then president of the General Electric Company and formerly director of our defense production. Although Mr. Wilson is said to have stated privately that he regrets this act, he has never publicly rescinded it.

The weaknesses which these incidents reveal in American thinking arise in large part from the rather widespread acceptance of the philosophy of pragmatism, which tries to see everything "new" as progressive and therefore desirable. Max Eastman, the noted author, put his finger on this blind spot when he stated that ninety per cent of those crying out for "free speech" for the seditious activities of the Communists are motivated by "a lingering feeling" that there is something progressive in Soviet Communism.[5]

In dealing with education, the average American must have a two-fold realization of the facts about Communist penetration. In order not to get into a panic, we must first recognize that the overwhelming majority of our educators are patriotic and desirous of serving America. When we consider the comparatively modest remuneration they receive for the important services they perform, we can pay tribute to their devotion to the United States. The second reality is the strong, aggressive, and persistent minority among our educators who are committed to the Communist cause and who serve repeatedly on Communist-front organizations. What is more to the point, they are well-organized, function secretly, and have influence beyond their numbers—even in official Washington. Nothing explains better why the rot of appeasement has extended as far as it has into higher and intelligent circles in our country.

[5] Address delivered at the Congress of the American Committee for Cultural Freedom, March 29, 1952, published in the *Brooklyn Tablet* of April 12, 1952.

# CHAPTER 8

# *Two Disasters*

Of the many calamities which have weakened the United States since V-J Day, the two most disastrous are the Red advances in China and the disintegration and division of Germany. Every aspect of American foreign policy depends upon the fate of China. The millions of expendable people in that huge country, placed at Stalin's disposal, constitute a permanent threat to all Asia and to the possibility of bringing on the "Battle for America." The events etched out so far concerning America's gift of China to the Soviet dictator must be developed further if the real significance of what occurred is to be understood.

Germany, with the greatest economic potential on the continent of Europe, was handed over light-heartedly to division, in which Soviet Russia received a considerable and highly productive area. At Soviet behests, organized devastation was carried on against German industry after the war, sapping it of the means of defense, while the initiative for the necessary unification of that country was permitted to slip into the hands of the Kremlin. As a result, in spite of billions of American taxpayers' money spent abroad, we have gained not much more than a foothold in Europe.

In 1948, former Vice President Henry A. Wallace produced a book, *Toward World Peace,* which gave a key to the first of these great disasters. It explains why we got into interminable Korean war and face the prospect of further American bloodshed in Asia. In a naïve estimate of the nature of Soviet Russia, which was shared by certain other American leaders, Mr. Wallace defends the extensive purges by Stalin in 1937-38 and champions the Kremlin's pact with Hitler in 1939. "From the standpoint of Russia's safety," wrote the former Vice President, "no one can say that Stalin did the wrong thing in agreeing to the pact with Hitler or in attacking Finland." As for the charge that in the "cold war" Soviet Russia had adopted a "tough and suspicious" attitude, Mr. Wallace declared that there was both a historic and immediate justification for all the Kremlin did.

From that miscalculation Wallace proceeded to another which has left a tragic mark upon the retreat of the United States before Soviet aggression. This had to do with the Chinese Communists and their relations with Moscow. Wallace denied flatly that Mao Tse-tung and his followers are "Russian agents" or that the Soviet Union would dominate China if the Communists defeated Chiang Kai-shek. He asserted forcefully that what had occurred in China and was in 1948 still moving toward the Communist seizure of power was not the result of any alleged "Russian infiltration." Further, he added, the Chinese Communists were in reality "agrarian reformers" and not Communists at all.

This considered judgment by a man who had been in the high councils of the nation in responsible positions, including that of being next in line to the chief executive, is significant. For it was he who, at a critical moment in 1944, was charged with the responsibility of a special mission to Soviet Siberia and China. The views he expressed so frankly were based on the actual delusion that finally determined American relations with China, and led to such tragic consequences.

It may be argued that in 1948 Mr. Wallace was a candidate for President on the ticket of the Progressive Party, which turned out to be dominated by the American Reds. It may also be said that he had been stripped of all official responsibility when his resignation as Secretary of Commerce was requested by the White House. These facts are all true, but the dominant fact which cannot be denied is that the United States could not have acted as it did in China without concurring in the views advocated by the former Vice President. It was only the lack of understanding of Soviet control of Mao Tse-tung and of the Soviet aim to dominate China that could have persuaded the American representatives at the Yalta Conference to grant Manchuria to Stalin. Manchuria, as the heart of industrial China, was especially necessary to a nation which had been stricken with civil war and the Japanese invasion. To give Manchuria to the Soviet dictatorship was equivalent in the United States to presenting the Chicago-Detroit-Pittsburgh area to the Kremlin. Only the belief that there had been no serious "Russian infiltration" of China and that there had been no large-scale activities by Soviet agents there could explain the acquiescence by the American State Department in Mao Tse-tung's proposal of a "coalition government" as the necessary "solution" of the Chinese difficulties.

We will recall that on January 1, 1945, Mao Tse-tung had publicly appealed to all the "allied" nations to request Chiang Kai-shek to consent to "a coalition." The Red leader asserted that "a coalition in the central gov-

ernment which is able to carry out democratic programs"
was a necessity. Immediately afterward, the American
Communists launched a big and successful campaign for
the ousting of all individuals critical of the Reds from both
China and the State Department. In the following November, after the forced resignation of General Patrick
Hurley as ambassador to China, General George Mar
shall was appointed as the special ambassador of the
President to that country. Upon his arrival in China,
General Marshall was presented by the Communists with
a truce proposal on the basis of the lines of the Communist armies and Chiang Kai-shek's troops as they existed at that time. Subsequent events showed that the
Communists had no intention of living up to such an
arrangement.

General Marshall arranged the truce, and furthermore
got Chiang Kai-shek to agree to a "constituent assembly"
which would bring the Communists into the government. The Communist International knew all about
"constituent assemblies" and how to handle them. Lenin
had originally raised the cry for such a body in Russia
and then had crushed by force all possibility of its functioning. Never had the Communists entered a "united
front" or "coalition" except for the purpose of destroying those with whom they "coalesced." Such a tactic was
officially explained in detail by Giorgi Dimitrov, General Secretary of the Communist International, at the
conclusion of his famous 1935 report on "the united
front." Dimitrov had stated that Communists could enter
such united fronts only for the purpose of achieving the
Soviet dictatorship and the rule of the Communist Party
in each country. This he appropriately termed a "Trojan
Horse" policy.

Since all of this was widely known in informed circles,

in giving directives to General Marshall the State Department could only have agreed to "coalition" proposals in the belief that there was no Soviet intervention in China. Even the White Paper of 1950, issued in defense of State Department policies in the Far East under the editorship of Dr. Philip Jessup, acquiesced in this viewpoint. By making Chiang Kai-shek the chief villain in the piece, it glossed over the long record of Soviet interference in Chinese affairs.

The "coalition" truce brought about by General Marshall was hailed by American Communists as a great victory. A leading editorial in the *Daily Worker* of February 2, 1946, entitled "A New Chance For China," began:

The people of China have a lot to cheer about in the agreement which Chiang Kai-shek has been forced to accept after the month-long conference with the Communist and other democratic parties. . . . The Communists' long fight against civil war, for a democratic coalition, and economic reconstruction is now being rewarded.

Of General Marshall's part in the proceedings the editorial stated:

It was the outcry of the American people against imperialist assistance to the Kuomintang which helped. That compelled General George C. Marshall to act differently from the former Ambassador, General Hurley.

Since the voice and acts of "the people," in Red parlance, are those expressions and drives conducted by the Communists themselves, this editorial testifies to the success of the Soviet fifth column and its campaigns. During 1945 it had conducted an unending battle for American agreement to "coalition" government in China. The center of this campaign had been the repeated Communist assertions that Soviet Russia was not intervening in any way in the Chinese scene and that the sole outside interference came from the United States. All of this had been climaxed by an official directive to all Communists, issued on November 19 by the Communist Party National Committee, which called for "an anti-imperialist campaign" on China. "Stop the reactionary intervention of the USA in China's internal affairs!" was the first battle cry.

Exactly one week later this directive had repercussions on the floor of the House of Representatives. Representative Hugh DeLacey of Washington, who was later identified as a Communist, delivered a stirring speech denouncing the United States as guilty of "dollar imperialism" in the Far East. "Quit China" was the slogan raised by DeLacey, and he was joined in the presentation of a resolution to that effect by five other representatives. These included the late John M. Coffee and Helen Gahagan Douglas of California.

Rallies were held and statements obtained in various cities from newspapermen and civic leaders that the United States should end its "intervention." The National Maritime Union, then under Communist control, threatened a national strike unless all GI's were returned at once, including specifically those in the Far East. The Committee for a Democratic Far Eastern Policy, a Communist front organized for the "quit China" campaign, issued statements by "noted citizens" attacking the United States for not abandoning Chiang Kai-shek. Prominent among those signing such absurd declarations was, of course, Frederick Vanderbilt Field (since jailed for defying the courts), at that time an active member of the executive committee of the Institute of Pacific Relations. His co-signers included, among others, Maxwell

Stewart of *The Nation,* Mrs. Edgar Snow, known professionally as Nym Wales, the Reverend Stephen Fritchman of the American Unitarian Association, Arthur Upham Pope of the Iranian Institute, and Gunther Stein. The last-named was listed in the statement as a "radio commentator"—in fact, as is now established, he was a Soviet espionage agent.

In order to arm the Communists and their fellow travelers with ammunition on "Russian non-intervention" and "American interference," a carefully written article appeared in the *Daily Worker* of December 15, 1945. This was written by Joseph Starobin, foreign editor of the *Daily Worker,* and therefore very active in Red international intrigue. He wrote: "The USSR is not intervening in China. The United States is, and will pay a heavy price for this policy as time goes on. The USSR remains in Manchuria only by agreement with the Central Government, and all Chinese know that the Red Army will withdraw." To this typical Red declaration, which of course has proved to be untrue, he added: "The United States is in China as a means of dominating the Central Government." Necessarily, Starobin concluded with a demand for "pressure for a democratic foreign policy by the people of the United States."

In the "quit China" campaign, the Reds were enormously helped by the timely flood of books by so-called "Far Eastern experts," which dominated the literary market during that momentous period. There was, to take an extreme example, Harrison Forman's *Report on Red China,* commended by the *Daily Worker* to its readers and ordered for wide promotion in a special directive from the New York State committee of the Communist Party. Then there was Gunther Stein's *The Challenge of Red China.* This was designated by Samuel Sillen, editor of the cultural page of the *Daily Worker,* as "this richly documented, masterfully organized book." Then, on December 3, 1945, the *Daily Worker* reviewed at great length *New Frontiers in Asia* by Philip Jaffe of *Amerasia* ill-fame and now identified by testimony as a Soviet espionage agent. In this connection, Joseph Starobin stated, as noted above:

The writers, experts, journalists—and even career diplomats in the State Department—are almost unanimous in their judgment of the reactionary character of the Kuomintang leaders, in their sympathy for the Chinese Communist program. . . . This has given rise to a virtual renaissance of American writing and thinking on the Far East.

Then Starobin furnished the comrades with a roll call of those who have received Communist approval in this field:

Philip Jaffe's book is the latest contribution of this judgment of the experts. It follows a remarkable outpouring of progressive literature about Asia in the last two years. There was Owen Lattimore's *Solution in Asia,* Kate Mitchell's study of India, and Kumar Goshal's work on the same subject. We have also had Lawrence K. Rosinger's *China's Crisis* and Andrew Roth's *Dilemma in Japan*—excellent statements from the younger men in the Far Eastern field. And then there were two eye-witness reports on the Chinese Communists by Harrison Forman and Gunther Stein.

These are the names, among others, which have paraded through the files and correspondence of the Institute of Pacific Relations, as promoting pro-Soviet policies in the Far East. Their works, each in its own way, contributed to the conditioning of public opinion that Soviet intervention in the Far East was nil while American imperialism was the guilty intruder. In November,

1946, Frederick Vanderbilt Field, in an important article in *Political Affairs,* cited perhaps the most influential of these authorities as follows: "The well-known liberal writer, Owen Lattimore, has characterized the role of America in the Far East a century ago as that of a 'hitch-hiking imperialism.' "

The widely spread propaganda that there was no "Russian infiltration" in China is one of the greatest hoaxes ever perpetrated on the American public. There is no factor more constant in the modern history of China than the continued interference by Soviet Russia through its agents in that country's life. Because of that interference, civil war harassed China for a quarter of a century. Lenin early emphasized the vital character of China in winning the world Soviet dictatorship. In one of his last articles, reviewing the world scene, as he had given it to the Second World Congress of the Comintern, Lenin stressed the fact that the Asiatic countries, and specifically China, could assure the victory of the Soviet dictatorship throughout the globe. "The result of the struggle," Lenin wrote, "will depend in the end on the fact that Russia, India, China, etc., constitute the gigantic majority of the population of the world."

Acting on this advice, the Russian Communists proceeded to carry their "revolution" into the large Asiatic country adjoining them. The Chinese Communist Party was formed in 1919, and made its formal public appearance two years later. Representatives of the Communist International, first Michael Borodin and then the Indian Communist, Manabendranath Roy, directed the new organization. On their heels came a host of others, including Heinz Neumann from Germany and Lominadze. The All-China Labor Congress was fostered by these Comintern agents, and a united front was established with Sun Yet-sen, who had risen to dominance by his drive for the "Three Principles of the People"—their livelihood, nationalism, and democracy. The most promising member of the united front, a rising follower of Sun Yat-sen by the name of Chiang Kai-shek, was sent to Moscow for military education.

So genuinely did the Russian Communist leaders consider Chiang Kai-shek to be their willing instrument that when he assumed the leadership in the Kuomintang against them in 1927, the Comintern officially denounced him as "a renegade" and a "traitor to the revolution." Nicholas Bukharin, then a leading member of the Politburo of the Communist Party of Soviet Russia, gave instructions immediately to the Chinese Communist Party as to how it should proceed. He ordered the Chinese Communists to operate within the Kuomintang in such a way as to split it wide open. (Published for the Communists of all countries in *International Press Correspondence* of July 14, 1927.) Bukharin's instructions were categorical, with the word "must" playing its usual prominent part. His hopes, and those of his colleagues, were expressed in the spring of 1927 by the executive committee of the Comintern, the ECCI, which had declared that the world was divided into two camps: "one, the Soviet Union and revolutionary China; the other, the whole of the capitalist world."

In an attempt to strengthen the Soviet fifth column on a broader scale, Moscow sent into China the American, Earl Browder, the Englishman, Tom Mann, and the Frenchman, Jacques Doriot. Their reports, appearing in the International Press Correspondence, indicate that their commission was to study the Chinese workers' movements in order to spread Communism among them.

But Chiang Kai-shek, educated in Moscow in Com-

munist tactics, insisted that the Soviet agents be withdrawn or expelled from China. When they did not move
fast enough, he arrested a number of them, including
Mrs. Borodin. The Reds were badly shattered and when
they attempted an insurrection in Canton, it was crushed.
For a moment it looked as though the hopes of the Kremlin were defeated. But the prize was too great to abandon the struggle—the goal was too rigidly laid out by
Lenin and Stalin.

By 1931, Moscow had discovered a new Red leader in
China. He was Mao Tse-tung, who had organized soviets
in Kiansi Province. Differing with Li Li-san, the Chinese
Communist leader chosen by the Comintern agents,
Mao Tse-tung went to Moscow and was personally designated by Stalin the Kremlin's chief emissary in China. He
was named General Secretary of the Chinese Communist
Party. A separate Soviet government was set up in China,
with Mao Tse-tung its official head, ruling over those dis-
tricts which the Chinese Red Army could maintain
against Chiang's Kuomintang forces. Shortly thereafter,
he made another pilgrimage to Moscow, this time to plan
with Stalin the famous Long March of the Chinese Communist troops from the south to the farthest northwest in
Shensi, where the "Chinese soviets" could set themselves
up nearer to Soviet Russia and in a much safer position.

From 1934 on, Mao Tse-tung was a symbol of Soviet
Russian intervention in China. Pleas in behalf of "the
Chinese Soviets," with demands that they be permitted
to exist and expand, were broadcast by Soviet Russian
agents all over the world. In marches, banners, and May
Day parades, the Communists everywhere spoke out for
Mao Tse-tung and his followers. He was the Kremlin's
chosen subordinate. The most competent aides were sent
him by the Comintern. Gerhart Eisler's sister, Ruth

Fischer, has testified that her brother was sent to China to purge the Chinese Communist Party and assure its absolute loyalty to Stalin. From the famous report of G-2, our military intelligence service in the Far East, we learn that as early as 1938 the Soviet Russian ambassador presented to Chiang Kai-shek as a major condition of "Soviet-Chinese understanding" the formation of a coalition government in China. This was seven years before the Chinese Reds raised that issue formally with the "allies."

On their side, the Chinese Communists expressed their adherence to Stalin. No American claiming to be a "Far Eastern expert" could after 1935 possibly have been deceived as to Stalin's plans for China. At the Seventh World Congress of the Communist International, held in Moscow in 1935, sixty-five national Communist parties, including the Chinese, enthusiastically declared that the Soviet Union is "the fatherland of the toilers of the whole world." It was at that conference that the noted resolution was adopted officially and solemnly proclaiming Stalin as the "leader, teacher, and friend of the proletariat and oppressed of the whole world." Led by the Chinese Communist Party, the representatives of the sixty-five Communist parties declared that under "the great and invincible banner of Marx, Engels, Lenin, and Stalin, Communism will triumph throughout the world." Further honor had been justly acquired by the Chinese Communists when, in an official greeting to the assembled Congress, they declared their faith in "the leadership of the man whose name has long since been inscribed in the pages of history, a man of deepest wisdom, unexampled courage, inexhaustible energy, unlimited love and devotion to the toiling people, of immortal deeds, the great Stalin." They added their solemn pledge to "facilitate the preparations for the decisive barricade fights for the Soviet Power through the world." This pledge they have fulfilled—at the cost of American lives in Korea.[1]

The myth of nonintervention by Soviet Russia in China is one of the most fatal in which American leadership has indulged. It has permitted the Chinese Communists to take over the major and most strategic area of the Far East, to attack the whole Western world through Korea and to put all Asia in jeopardy. If persisted in, it will permit Stalin to consolidate his control of the millions there, training expendable armies for assaults upon Hawaii and the West Coast. In spite of Korea, the myth lingers on in America. In 1950 and 1951, the American people were treated to a new outbreak of articles in various publications, describing Mao Tse-tung as a different type of Communist from Stalin. One "Far Eastern expert," Theodore White, who in 1946, as co-author of *Thunder Out of China,* had done his share in the promotion of Chinese Communists, has suggested that, with our boys dying in Korea, we should be "patient" with Mao Tse-tung and give him time to work out his orientation regarding Moscow.

Secretary of State Acheson did, it is true, finally declare in 1951 that Soviet Russia was guilty of aggression in China. But this statement, like so many others, was not reflected in American policy, since Great Britain was not pressed to withdraw recognition of our Chinese Red enemy. As a matter of fact, according to Beverley Baxter, Member of Parliament, Great Britain recognized Red

---

[1] *International Press Correspondence,* agency of the Communist International, Vol. 15, No. 33, Aug. 8, 1935, page 857. The records of the proceedings of the first session of the Seventh Congress of the Communist International.

China with the tacit approval of our own State Department.

The most pronounced success, at least temporarily, that the United States had had in the Far East is in the conclusion of the peace treaty with Japan. This success is largely due to an occupation administration which kept its eyes open to the existence of Soviet intervention and thwarted the Kremlin in an outstanding manner.

The occupation authorities in Japan carried through their work despite the widespread campaign by the American Communists and fellow travelers against General Douglas MacArthur. In addition to the charges that MacArthur favored a "soft peace" and was the ally of the Japanese industrialists, there were accusations that he violated "the civil liberties" of the Japanese people. This allegation was refuted by a tour of investigation made by Roger N. Baldwin, director of the American Civil Liberties Union, who declared that civil rights were being scrupulously observed by the occupation authorities. Also, John Foster Dulles, who arranged the final treaty with Japan, said of General MacArthur on a television program February 15, 1952: "I think that he did a perfectly amazing job in Japan. There's never in history been an occupation which has been as fruitful as that was."

But there was still another factor in Japan to contend with. John Carter Vincent, of the State Department, pursued a policy in Japan based on the "tough peace" idea—a policy which Eugene C. Dooman, his predecessor at the China desk, has testified to the Senate Subcommittee helped the Communist campaign. John K. Emerson recommended in a report to the State Department that the civilian government of Japan be made up only of Communists, since the Red group was the only "democratic" force there. The Soviet Russian representatives also sought repeatedly to dominate the occupation. But all such proposals were rejected by General MacArthur, and consequently appeasement did not mar the American occupation of Japan.

In contrast, we are presented with the huge difficulties confronting the United States in Germany. With the surrender of Poland to Stalin, the German scene offers a second international disaster for America. Acquiescense by the United States in the idea of the partition of Germany was a serious blow to the very cause for which we had fought the war. The Soviet occupation of a large part of Germany has given the Kremlin the opportunity to take the initiative in the outcry for "unification." Within the United States, the Soviet drive to get unification on its own terms was given new impetus at the Fifteenth National Convention of the Communist Party. In his report as acting general secretary, Gus Hall made this objective for Germany the second great immediate task of the American Reds, the first being the assurance of a Communist victory in the Far East through recognition of Red China. In this directive to the Communists in this country and their allies, Hall, of course, echoed the instructions of the Cominform and the Kremlin.

As late as October 5, 1951, the Cominform organ was making the battle for "a united democratic peace-loving Germany" a major obligation of its followers throughout the world. The Cominform directive is perfectly clear about what it is aiming at in all this. The center of its "united, democratic" German nation would be the German Democratic Republic, the Soviet satellite government of East Germany. "The establishment of the German Democratic Republic," it declares, "was significant not only for the German people; it is also of immense international significance. J. V. Stalin defined this great historic step taken by the German people as a turning point in the history of Europe." And then to bring out more pointedly the Red objective, Stalin is quoted as saying "that the existence of a peace-loving, democratic Germany, side by side with the existence of a peace-loving Soviet Union" would rebuff "the world imperialists" in Europe.

The United States is thus facing the possibility of another Korea in the heart of Europe, only now on a much more gigantic scale. The aim of unification for a truly democratic Germany, which should have been initiated by the United States, is now fraught with obstacles. These stem from American policy toward Germany during and since World War II, which was based on the Morgenthau Plan. This plan, as we now know, was conceived and developed by the late Harry Dexter White (formerly Under Secretary of the Treasury), who has been named by Whittaker Chambers and Elizabeth Bentley as furnishing information to Soviet spy rings. The very first item in the Morgenthau Plan was the prostration of Germany through partition, with the United States excluded from any occupational authority. This would have quickly turned the defeated country over to Soviet control. With that initial folly went the proposal for destroying the industrial plants and economy of Germany, thereby turning it into a purely agricultural country, and the sanction for German labor to be used in other lands. This policy, obviously designed to render impotent Moscow's chief competitor in industrial and military strength in Europe, was approved by President Roosevelt and Winston Churchill at Quebec.

The American Communists were decidedly vocal in supporting the idea of the Morgenthau Plan. In a leading editorial of February 19, 1945, the *Daily Worker* declared that "none shall escape judgment." It called not only for "ruthless punishment of all war criminals" but also for "full restitution by the enemy." In this restitution, it included specifically the necessity of deporting German workers into other lands as part of "the reparations." The Red paper assailed the criticism made by William Green of the American Federation of Labor, when he stated that the use of German labor in other lands, as proposed by the plan, was nothing more than "slave labor." "These words," declared the *Daily Worker,* "are comfort only to dying fascism." Thereafter, this became a slogan of the Soviet fifth column here. Any consideration for the German people on the part of the United States was labelled as "yielding to fascism." In this way a considerable section of American opinion was swayed, and while the Morgenthau Plan did not go through in full force and effect, its spirit continued, as subsequent American decisions show, including the Potsdam Agreement.

Partition became a definite policy, with Soviet Russia receiving a larger territory than its military advances justified, despite the protests attributed to General George S. Patton.

These commitments were made, strengthening Soviet power enormously, even though the Kremlin had indicated quite clearly by previous actions that its single motive was the advancement of its own ambitions. The Communists, at a critical moment in German history, had aided the Nazis in the Reichstag and elsewhere in putting down the Social Democrats and other German democratic parties. In entering upon the Hitler-Stalin Pact, V. M. Molotov, speaking for the Soviet dictatorship, declared that "fascism is a matter of taste." At that time he had stated also that Soviet Russia stood for "a strong Germany," which could, then, mean only a strong Nazi Germany.

That statement was apparently forgotten in many American official circles, and the Communist-inspired charge that anyone proposing a constructive program for Germany was "favoring fascism" became general. The United States agreed to the corridor around the American sector in Berlin, thereby giving Soviet forces a stranglehold on the former capital. At Potsdam, the American representatives agreed with Stalin that there should be no "remilitarization" of Germany, which it was clear from past events the Soviet dictatorship in its sector would ignore. Agreement was also reached on the dismantling of non-military industrial plants, as well as those engaged in military production, and their possible removal outside Germany. This, in fact, gave sanction to the looting of all the countries that Soviet Russia occupied, including the removal of industrial plants from Germany. This was particularly unfortunate because of the key position it occupies geographically and economically in Europe.

The United States had walked into the Soviet trap and the Kremlin was quick to take advantage of what had been done. In an address to the German people, the Soviet Foreign Minister, V. M. Molotov piously proclaimed that the Soviet government did not approve of "ill-treatment" of the German people. Whereupon James F. Byrnes, then Secretary of State, made his famous trip to Stuttgart, where he solemnly declared that neither did we. It was clear, by his words, that the United States was on the defensive.

American economic aid to the West German [Bonn] Republic did much to promote a feeling of friendship

toward America. The repression in East Germany by the
Soviets contrasted unfavorably with the growing freedom permitted under the West German government.
Still, the seed the Communists planted continues to
sprout. Today "unification" is a vital and disturbing
issue on the German scene. The Soviet-controlled People's Chamber of the German Democratic Republic, late
in 1951, called upon all the German people to establish
"mutual understanding" among Germans "against the
criminal plans of the aggressor." With East Germany
completely under Soviet military control, the Soviet satellite arrogantly demanded that West Germany must not
be armed. To further this proposal, the satellite government proposed to the Bonn Federal Parliament that an
all-German meeting be held for the purpose of calling "a
national assembly." This body would establish "a united,
democratic, and peace-loving Germany," would "demand
speedy signing of a peace treaty with Germany, and the
withdrawal of all occupation troops." Although the
Bonn Federal Parliament rejected this proposal, the
Soviet fifth column in Germany is not daunted. The
Moscow weekly, *New Times,* on October 3, 1951, reports "a strong tide of protest [against the American occupation authorities]" started throughout West Germany.
"The provocative actions of the occupation authorities
are arousing general indignation," it adds. The immediate incidents noted are the blowing up of certain bridges
for military defensive purposes. It is clear, from the reports in the *New Times,* that these acts of "provocation"
are, in fact, performed by Communists.

The character of the appeal which is being made to
the Germans is indicated by the concluding sentences in
the *New Times* report: "Alarm is growing in the hearts
of millions of Germans as they hear the stamp of soldiers

boots and the military commands in English and German, which are again to be heard in the exercise grounds and in the former Nazi barracks of Western Germany."

This is definitely addressed to the war-weariness of the people of West Germany, and conveniently ignores the Soviet preparations in the East and Soviet readiness to use Nazi military establishments or even personnel for its own ends. A striking example of this tactic is Rumania. The Soviet occupation forces of that country made use of many of Hitler's leading collaborators against the democratic section of the population. In the bloody persecutions which followed, these former Nazi collaborators were of great aid in setting up a Soviet Rumania.

Today the fear of a war involving Europe is held before the German people as a threat. Thus the *New Times* declares that the "words of warning uttered by the People's Chamber of the German Democratic Republic," including its "earnest appeal for the unification of the country . . . were received with such attention and support in all parts of Germany."

Cominform agents are now spreading the word that any new military formation in the Bonn Republic will be "a revival of the fascist army." They are widely denouncing "the dismemberment of Germany, brought about by the British and French imperialists." They call for "struggle waged by the progressive forces of the German people" against these so-called imperialists.

In raising the German question once more, the American Comunists have applied the term "fascist armies" not only to troops being organized in West Germany but also to the forces under General Dwight D. Eisenhower in other European countries.

Adequate preparation was made by Gerhart Eisler, writing in the *Daily Worker* under his assumed name of

Hans Berger, in a series of articles published as a book, *The Lesson of Germany*, in November, 1945, by the International Publishers, a Communist concern. In that book Eisler portrays Germany as "a festering source of danger for the rest of the world." But Eisler goes on to something more significant when he asserts that the way to rid Germany of its danger is to extirpate the classes which made for war. This is precisely the formula used by the Communists in regard to Japan. And their definition of the "classes" that must be extirpated is so broad as to leave the cause of "democracy and peace" in the end in the hands of the Reds alone. Thus it is that Eisler advised his American comrades that a Soviet Germany is the only possible goal.

It is obvious that the Soviet dictatorship and its agents are planning such future turmoil in Germany as will discredit the United States. The cry for "peace" is a powerful one, especially among people who have experienced the horrors of modern war. The desire for unification is also close to the hearts of the German people.

It is true the American, British, and French governments have expressed the desire for unification several times, and the West German Government at Bonn has repeatedly stated this aim. But as Jack Raymond, special correspondent of the New York *Times,* wrote on January 6, 1952, from Bonn:

It is typical of the Communists that they are forever on the offensive with spectacular, albeit meaningless statements on German unity, whereas the Western Allies and the West Germans are forever on the defense. Bringing the issue of all German elections before the United Nations [as happened in late 1951] is so isolated an example of Western initiative in this field that its effect noticeably is wearing off.

As evidence of how "the Eastern Communists forever keep the question of German unity in the public eye," Raymond notes: "Recent examples are the trip to Moscow by the Reverend Martin Niemöller; the visit to East Berlin by former Chancellor Josef Wirth, West German resident; the meeting in Berlin of several West German politicians and most recently, the announcement of a draft law for all German elections sponsored by the East German Communists."

As a continuation of the hesitancy and paralysis of "letting the dust settle" in the Far East, the American State Department is pursuing a course in regard to Germany that may prove fatal for us in continental Europe. In stressing that the road ahead in Germany permits "no time for patchwork or half measures," Dr. Friedrich Baerwald, a well-known economist, declared upon his recent return from Europe that unification was of the utmost importance. Referring to the need by the United States to emphasize "free elections looking to German unity," Dr. Baerwald wrote: "We cannot allow these negotiations to be carried on in such a way that the Communists give the impression of holding better cards than we do (their alleged interest in German unification) while we, by showing disinterest or even fear, trump our own aces."

Not long after these words were written, the Kremlin took the West again by surprise in proposing a "unified" and armed Germany, which would be outside the orbit of the North Atlantic Treaty Organization. This contains obvious dangers, since it would be a plan under which the Soviet sector would have a great advantage. It would also prevent Germany from being a real ally of the Western nations. But this proposal does call for a counter-move by the United States in a great call to the German people to oppose Soviet rule as a guarantee of a genuinely independent and united nation.

The position of the United States in Germany, like our position in the Far East, is untenable because of a basic error in American thinking. That error is the continuing faith that Soviet Russia was, is, or might become, something other than it is; that the dictatorship can be persuaded to keep its word; and that firm steps are not necesssary to halt its ambitions. There is no assurance in recent months that this error does not linger on.

# CHAPTER 9

# *Two Illusions*

Twenty thousand Communists and their friends gathered at Madison Square Garden on the night of November 14, 1945, to hear Dean Acheson, then Under Secretary of State, declare that "for the peace of the world" the Soviet Union must have "friendly governments along her borders." (For "friendly," read Soviet-dominated.) This declaration of American policy sealed the fate of Eastern Europe and China, for it publicly proclaimed official American acquiescence in Stalin's moves in those regions. Widely published in the press, it evoked but a very few comments to the effect that such a "peace" would lead to aggression, organized murder, and the general terror prevailing behind the Iron Curtain.

The declaration was made, appropriately, before a mass meeting held under the auspices of the National Council of American-Soviet Friendship, a group which a few years later was to be labeled subversive by the Attorney General of the United States. Even at that time, its control by the Communist Party was quite evident. For weeks in advance the meeting was played up by the *Daily Worker,* with the "Red Dean" of Canterbury, Hewlett Johnson, as the star performer. It was well known that the bulk of the audience, at every meeting called by the National Council since its inception was composed of those rallied by the *Daily Worker*. It was equally well known that most of the thousands assembled in Union Square only five days before to denounce the United States Government and demand that it "quit China," were the same people who assembled to hear Mr. Acheson. Speaking from the same platform with Acheson, the Communist Paul Robeson placed the full responsibility for future peace on the American nation. If this country and the United Nations, he said, "truly want peace and security, let them fulfill the hopes of common peoples everywhere. . . . Let them work together to accomplish on a world-wide scale precisely the kind of democratic association of free peoples which characterizes the Soviet Union today."

Corliss Lamont, chairman of the National Council of American-Soviet Friendship, gave voice to a similar fiction about China. "The Soviets stand for non-intervention in the complex Chinese situation," stated Lamont. "It would be a great step forward if the American government would support Soviet Russia in its hands-off policy. . . ."

It was in this meeting, at the crucial moment when Soviet Russia was beginning her warfare against the United States, that those two illusions which were to prove so tragic for us were promulgated. The belief that the Soviet Union would maintain peace if given control of "bordering countries," that it had not intervened in China, and that it was a model democracy, formed the backdrop for the two chief illusions that now cloud the minds of Americans.

The first illusion, implicit in Mr. Acheson's words, was that the world-wide conspiratorial apparatus of the Communists is weak. Otherwise he could hardly have encouraged Soviet infiltration into "neighboring nations" as he did. Nor would he have addressed one of the leading Communist-front organizations, created by the Kremlin as a part of its infiltration policy in every country of the world under the name "Friends of Soviet Russia." Almost at the very moment when he spoke, the *Daily Worker* was denouncing the United States as guilty of "atomic blackmail," and demanding that all our atomic secrets be handed over to Soviet Russia. It was insisting that the United States surrender Korea while Soviet agents remained there. It was crying out for the withdrawal of all American troops from the Far East. Its aggressive psychological warfare within the United States, carried on to befog the American mind, was plainly evident.

This psychological warfare waged by the Soviet fifth column within our borders has been the most decisive factor in shaping our foreign policy up to the present hour. An examination of the Communist organs which have given directives since 1935 will reveal startlingly how Soviet objectives have come to be accepted by dominant segments of the American leadership. And in no period was this success more pronounced than in the days following Mr. Acheson's fateful speech before a leading Communist-front organization.

So great have been the resulting setbacks to the United States in foreign fields that six years after that event, a revamped Psychological Strategy Board is considering how to offset Soviet propaganda—in other countries. The New York *Times,* which has not been unfriendly to many proposals linked with appeasement, makes a series of admissions in signalizing what it terms "a groping effort to define United States aims." In the *Times* of December 10, 1951, we read: "For more than thirty years, the Soviet Union has been expanding the empire of Lenin and Stalin. It is an empire that has been infiltrated into men's minds in the most calculating way, under the influence of Moscow's opiate for the masses—propaganda."

This does not, however, underscore the basic reality—that Soviet propaganda within the United States has been most effective upon developments throughout the world. Nor does it emphasize the companion reality that this success has flowed from deeds of appeasement by leading officials acting under the influence, direct or indirect, of such propaganda. We cannot put the burden for Soviet success upon "the masses."

George E. Sokolsky, in his syndicated column of December 10, 1951, brings an instance of this sort to public attention. At the San Francisco Conference which endorsed the treaty with Japan, Nationalist China was excluded. This was done, Mr. Sokolsky charges, by agreement with John Foster Dulles, representing the State Department. China was excluded even though Soviet Russia was permitted to be present. As a consequence Nationalist China, our ally for years, and Communist China, which was at war with us, "were put on a basis of equality."

As an excuse for this act, which encouraged Great Britain in its recognition of Red China, it was agreed that Japan was to enter into separate negotiations with Nationalist China "and would negotiate a bi-lateral agreement with them." It now appears, as George Sokolsky has observed, "that no such agreement will be signed," and he sees in this the earmarks of "a first-class doublecross."

In objection to this, it may be noted that Premier Yoshida of Japan, in January, 1952, announced his willingness to enter into an agreement with the Chinese Nationalist Government on Formosa. But we must not overlook his awareness that the United States Senate had declared by a vote of 91-to-0 against recognition of Red China, and that if Japan were to indicate any tendency in that direction now it would kill or delay the Japanese peace treaty. Since Yoshida's words have restricted his relations with Nationalist China to Formosa, and would of course preclude any agreement prior to the vote on the Japanese peace treaty in the Senate, the door is still open for Japanese recognition of Red China. Since Dean Rusk, former Assistant Secretary of State, was the special representative of the State Department in consultations with Yoshida, that department can scarcely be ignorant of these realities. The possibility of close relations between Japan and Red China thus remains a grave danger, particularly when we recall that the will of the Senate was rebuffed in excluding Nationalist China from the San Francisco Conference. There is the possibility, though we have no proof of it, that Stalin wanted us to sign the treaty with Japan, and that the public opposition put up by his delegate at San Francisco, and "squelched" by Acheson, was a calculated maneuver.

No propaganda initiated by the United States in other countries will register in any measure as long as deeds of this character make nations and peoples uncertain of our fidelity. The unwillingness of the State Department to persuade Great Britain to withdraw recognition of Red China encourages the tendency in Japan toward appeasement of Mao Tse-tung's regime. All this constitutes, whether adopted consciously with that purpose or not, a yielding within the United States to the outcries of the Communist-fronters, the most adroit feature of the Soviet psychological warfare within our borders.

This is no reflection on the personnel of the revised Psychological Strategy Board. Its new director, Dr. Raymond B. Allen, when president of the University of Washington, showed a lively awareness of the Red threat in educational institutions. Its chairman, General Walter Bedell Smith, in a book on his ambassadorship to Moscow, revealed a familiarity with the philosophy of Lenin and Stalin that was refreshing. But no psychological warfare abroad will be successful if it is constantly impeded by successful Soviet infiltration or influence upon governing and opinion-making agencies in the United States.

Proof of this influence appears in a survey by the New York *Times* of what has happened up to date. After six years of Stalin's World War III, says the *Times:* "United States policy-makers realize now that subjugation by the weapons of fear, hatred, and revolutionary activity can decide the fate of nations as effectively as military action." The newspaper adds: "They are aware belatedly that the Soviet Union could win the world without itself engaging in war." It admits that the United States has only appealed to the world "haltingly" in the past. And it even raises the question whether "at this late date" American ingenuity can quickly enough offset the Soviet ideological maneuvers.

What these admissions fail to disclose is the real crux of the problem: our psychological warfare abroad will fail of its effect so long as our policy-makers fail to recognize the results of Soviet psychological warfare at home. So long as our policies and the men executing them yield to the propaganda directed by the Soviet fifth column in our midst, their work is weakened all along the line. This is dramatized by the State Department's blindness throughout more than six crucial years to the unfitness of John Stewart Service as an American diplomat. On

December 13, 1951, Mr. Service was discharged by order of President Truman's top Loyalty Review Board for an act which he committed *six years and eight months before*. This act was the delivery by him of important State Department documents to Philip Jaffe, editor of the Communist magazine, *Amerasia*, since identified before both the Tydings and McCarran committees as a Soviet espionage agent. Service was at last discharged only after the Federal Loyalty Review Board found that there existed "a reasonable doubt" as to his loyalty.

To highlight the blindness of this procedure, Service's record is worth recounting briefly. He was one of the advisers to General Joseph Stilwell, whose pro-Communist sympathies went so far that even the Communists finally decided he had overplayed his hand. When Stilwell was removed as commander of the American forces in China, Mr. Service became an adviser to Major General Patrick J. Hurley, our Ambassador to China. When General Hurley was forced to resign, he accused Service of being part of a clique of "left wingers" who sabotaged his work. Service was called home in 1945 for "important duties at the State Department," thus receiving commendation rather than censure.

A few weeks later the Federal Bureau of Investigation linked Service with the theft of 1700 confidential documents, some of them marked "top secret," from the Office of Strategic Services, the Office of War Information, and the State Department, in the *Amerasia* case. Service was definitely proven to have conveyed "very secret" documents, as he himself described them, to Philip Jaffe and Andrew Roth, both identified under oath as Communist agents. While Jaffe pleaded guilty, and was fined $2500, Service weathered the storm, and all the others involved went scot-free, except Emmanuel S.

Larsen, State Department specialist on Far Eastern affairs, who was fined $500. Indeed, Service was not only reinstated, but commended and presented with an official apology by the State Department. From that time until 1951, Service underwent seven hearings on his loyalty before the State Department's loyalty review board. Each time he was declared guiltless.

When in 1950 Service appeared before the special Senate Investigating Committee headed by Senator Tydings, he admitted that in conferences with Jaffe he had handed official documents to the *Amerasia* editor. But he pleaded that the papers were not too important and that he had "tired of being an errand boy for Philip Jaffe." The Tydings Committee again cleared him and said only that he had been indiscreet.

It is significant that after a number of charges and hearings, and prior to the Tydings investigation, Service was appointed consul at New Delhi, India. It is said that he requested this appointment, which placed him in a most strategic position in view of a possible aggression by Stalin through Tibet. To place a man of such flagrantly doubtful loyalty in so important a post was an advertisement of our weakness in opposing Soviet aggression. It indicated an attitude toward Soviet ruthlessness which could not possibly produce either acts or propaganda strong enough to defeat the Kremlin's widespread aggressions and falsehoods. It served notice that some of our men in the diplomatic field, which the Communists regard as a field of warfare, were either ineffective or on the Soviet side.

Another instance arises from the New York *Times* articles themselves. It is mentioned in one article that the first choice for director of our psychological warfare was Mark Ethridge, publisher of the Louisville *Courier*

*Journal*. Now, Mr. Ethridge is a leading citizen of Kentucky and his paper enjoys the prestige of having been edited by Henry Watterson. But the Louisville *Courier-Journal* has in recent years been committed to a general policy of appeasement, and has vigorously and repeatedly defended the "whitewash" of Service and others by the Tydings Committee. In the fall of 1951, the Louisville *Courier-Journal* denounced me as a "professional ex-Communist" and "professional witness." It added that "the microphone-happy Louis Budenz who, apparently long since having run out of knowledge, seems resolved to protect his role by whatever it takes of innuendo."

Any responsible inquiry by the editors of the *Courier-Journal* or by Mr. Ethridge would have disclosed that I have frequently refused to testify in Communist cases. I believe and have stated that the ex-Communist best exposes Stalin's conspiracy by writing and speaking directly to the American people. Inquiry would also have disclosed that the charges in the Louisville *Courier-Journal* are the stock in trade of the Communists. They have been repeated continually in recent years by the *Daily Worker*. They are quite obviously an effort on its part to intimidate possible government witnesses, so that they will either defy the courts by eluding subpoenas or perjure themselves on behalf of the party and its associates. If Mr. Ethridge and his editors were unable to distinguish Red propaganda from the truth here at home, his fitness to combat such propaganda in other lands is certainly questionable. And this is the case, no matter with what good will he might go into the job. Yet we are informed that the only reason he was not chosen as director of this delicate activity is that he insisted on more discretion and power than was first allotted to the undertaking.

One of the favorite methods of the Reds in this country is the old device of denouncing as "fascism" any attempt to curb their conspiracy. A slight variation was proffered in the October 1951 issue of *Political Affairs*. Here it was made clear that the cry of "McCarthyism" is also to be used by the Communists and their friends as a means to parry any attacker or criticism. Vito Marcantonio, chairman of the Red-ruled Labor Party, is quoted with approval in describing McCarthyism as "the Frankenstein created by Truman." The article cites with satisfaction a number of instances in which the Communist cry of "fascism" has been taken up by groups far out beyond the periphery of the party. The Reds also pointed out that this campaign against "fascism" and the "police state" has its echoes in opinion-making agencies, and tends to affect official policy. *Political Affairs* boasts that even President Truman called the McCarran Internal Securty Act "totalitarian," just as the Communists do when demanding its repeal as a thrust at their "freedom" to undermine the United States.

The Reds assiduously spread the notion that "by its very nature, the Soviet Union cannot engage in aggressive war." As a socialist nation, where there is no exploitation of man by man, Soviet Russia can take control of other nations only to "liberate" them. Soviet foreign policy can therefore be only a "policy of peace." While this oft-repeated argument, emphasized in all leading Communist documents, does not reach out into wider fields in quite that sophisticated form; it finds an echo in the belief widely adhered to that there can be "peaceful co-operation" between the Soviet Union and the United States. Such a belief, completely in contradiction to the Red objective of world conquest, leads to the illusions that Soviet Russia will some day accept a genuine disarmament proposal, and that a truce established in Korea on the 38th parallel will be something besides an armed interlude, and may even lead to peace. These illusions divert us from taking the firm stand against Soviet aggression which would encourage the peoples of the world and lead to real peace.[1]

All these weaknesses in American policy, which are getting us entangled deeper and deeper in World War III, arise, as I said, from a lack of understanding of the nature and strength of the Soviet fifth column. The "picket-line Communist" is still the general conception of the typical party member, instead of the well-manicured influential gentleman on the type of Alger Hiss. This conception is cultivated by the Communists themselves who constantly represent their "movement" as of and for "the masses" and who keep their most effective agents carefully concealed. The Communist Party is frequently referred to in the press as possessing "only 55,000 members," although it is sometimes added that there are 500,000 "sympathizers." This sort of remark overlooks a warning by J. Edgar Hoover, director of the FBI, that these "sympathizers" are among the most valuable assets the party has. It also fails to note that a large number of them are actual Communists, "under discipline" but protected from legal jeopardy by having no cards or other marks of membership. Of course, today, when the party has put itself on a complete war footing, even the rank and filers have no such marks of membership.

The illusion of Communist weakness within the

---

[1] The arguments in regard to the Soviet "peace" policy are published so frequently in the organ of the Cominform, *For a Lasting Peace, For a People's Democracy,* and in the official theoretical organ of the Communist Party of the United States, *Political Affairs,* that I can give only a blanket reference to these publications. Consultation of their issues of 1950, 1951, and 1952 will suffice.

United States also ignores the key positions into which
the Stalinists have penetrated. Measured by Red standards, one Alger Hiss is worth more than 500,000 undis-
ciplined and loosely organized members. By his advice to
official Washington, Hiss aided in giving Stalin 600,000,-
000 people and untold resources. An analysis of the
famous or infamous Ware cell in Washington, exposed
by the careful questioning of Richard Nixon in the
House Committee on Un-American Activities in 1948,
would reveal how much a few key persons can accomplish. In addition to Hiss, other members of the cell included: Lee Pressman, who was counsel to the Congress
of Industrial Organizations and therefore a power in
Washington; Nathan Witt, who was secretary and counsel for the first National Labor Relations Board; and
John Abt, who after occupying various government posts
became counsel for the Amalgamated Clothing Workers
of America, which gave him entry into many official
circles. Other members of the cell were in government
offices and were engaged in espionage work. Thus a
handful of men as advisers, consultants, and contact
sources with those in official positions, became a very
considerable power in the land.

As leader of the conspiracy in the United States for
many years, Earl Browder sought diligently to nurture
this illusion of Red weakness in our country. He always
referred to "our party" as "a weak party," but in national committee meetings he described "our influence"
as great and growing. Secret testimony to this "influence"
was given by Robert Minor, Browder's right-hand man,
at the party sessions of 1945 which demoted Browder.
Minor stated that the falling Red chief had held secret
conferences with six senators. This assertion was deleted
from any printed records of the sessions, but the Com-

munists have never denied it, though I have quoted it in speech and writing many times over. Publicly this "influence" is registered in the continued support given by outstanding Americans to the National Council of American-Soviet Friendship, not only during World War II but also long after. Such men of standing as former Senator Claude Pepper of Florida continued public co-operation with this group even after the "cold war" had warmed up to a very marked extent. In this way the party's influence impeded the taking of a firm stand by the United States against Soviet tactics.

Nothing better illustrates our underestimation of the strength and techniques of the Soviet fifth column than the State Department's granting of free entry to Soviet agents under the guise of diplomatic immunity. This was brought to national attention by Senator Herbert R. O'Conor on the floor of the Senate in the latter part of 1951. The Maryland Senator revealed that from July, 1947 to March, 1951, visas totaling 3,616 in number were issued to aliens in diplomatic status to enter the United States from Iron Curtain countries. Among these he charged were a considerable number of Soviet espionage agents. One of these was a spy identified as Colonel Otto Biheler, military and air attaché at the Czechoslovak Embassy. Since his admission to the United States in August, 1948, Biheler had engaged in the procurement of information on atomic energy, the uranium stockpile, bacteriological and chemical warfare, and many other key military secrets. Another spy admitted to this country through the intervention of the Secretary of State, was Jari Stary, second secretary of the Czechoslovak delegation to the United Nations. Sworn testimony indicates, Senator O'Conor charged, that Stary had never been in diplomatic service prior to his assignment here, and that both he and his wife were part of the Soviet espionage apparatus. They were sent here to engage in such work.

Still another person involved in the Senator's charges was an alleged correspondent at the United Nations, an Egyptian citizen, Miss Marcell Hitschmannova. This woman had been here on brief permits since 1946, on her statement that she came to visit a friend, one Ruth Gruber, in New York City. This is the Ruth Gruber whose employment in the office of the Secretary of the Interior, Harold Ickes, was specifically terminated in 1941, by a vote of the House of Representatives charging her with "Communist sympathies." Although many other divisions of the government, including the Immigration and Naturalization Service, and even the Security Division of the State Department, have objected strongly to Miss Hitschmannova's continued residence here, the Secretary of State has intervened on each occasion. As a result, she has remained here on continuing permits for six years, although according to Senator O'Conor it was well known that she had acted in Egypt on behalf of the Soviet intelligence service. In 1946 she was in close contact with a Soviet agent who was engaged in a conspiracy to purloin United States government documents.

The State Department's continual defense of these agents is an open invitation to Soviet espionage in this country. It also blindly overlooks the service performed by such aliens as channels of communication between Moscow and the Communist organization in the United States.

Nothing illustrates more clearly the impact of this illusion of Red conspiratorial weakness than the present ironic scene in the United Nations, where the United States is being arraigned by Soviet Russia for subversive activities in the nations under satellite regimes. It has not even occurred to the United States to bring similarly challenging charges against the Soviet Union for its notorious fifth column here and in every other country.

The second major illusion causing weakness in America's reaction to Soviet aggression is the belief that the Soviet regime is much stronger economically and militarily than it really is. This also has been systematically propagated by the Communists under directions from Moscow. This great propaganda asset to the Kremlin may be illustrated by an article of Palmiro Togliatti, general secretary of the Communist Party of Italy, in a contribution to the Cominform's organ of December 21, 1949, entitled "Stalin's Cause Is Invincible." Here is a sample of it: "The Lenin teaching on imperialism and on the possibility of building socialism in one country, which are closely interrelated, were further clarified and developed by Stalin. Without this, Stalin's confident and successful work *in transforming the Socialist State into the greatest world power* . . . would be unthinkable." (Italics are mine.)

This chant, echoed throughout all countries, that the Soviet dictatorship is the "greatest world power," is designed primarily to frighten the United States from taking any decisive stand against Communist expansion. It was set in motion by Stalin shortly after the close of World War II. In his election address of February, 1946, Stalin declared that "the Red Army is that same army which routed completely the German Army—the terror of all armies of peace-loving states." [2] Thus the big role of the American GI's in saving Soviet Russia through the Second Front is brushed aside. The Communists, taking this cue from their "leader, teacher, and guide," have re-

[2] The authorized English translation of this election address was published in full in the *Daily Worker* of February 11, 1946.

peated over and over again that "the decisive factors" in Hitler's defeat were the Soviet economy and the Red Army. This is not mere braggadocio; it is calculated propaganda and has its effect. Being stepped up gradually, it finally reached the point where the Communists claimed that Soviet Russia had been the largest factor in the defeat not only of Nazi Germany but of "Fascist-militarist Japan" as well. This statement was solemnly and successfully made by Alexander Bittelman, among others, in *Political Affairs* of November 1950.

As chief theoretician of the American Communist Party, Bittelman's purpose in describing these "invincible achievements"—which give no credit to the United States or to our American soldiers—was to make it appear that inevitably "a socialist world is coming into existence." This new "world" is headed by the Soviet Union, the giant which had outdone all other fighters in the recent war. The Communists of the world are given the same lead by the *New Times* of Moscow in its issue of January 1, 1950. None other than V. M. Molotov is there quoted as saying that from a frontal war between the United States and Soviet Russia, there would ensue "the destruction of the entire system of world imperialism," that is, the conquest of the United States and the triumph of the world Soviet dictatorship.

This legend of the "invincible" power of the Soviet economy and Red Army was brought up to date at the Fifteenth National Convention of the American Communist Party, held secretly in December, 1950. Attention was given on a large scale to the fright inspired in leading American circles by the might of Soviet Russia. The American leaders "are thrown into deep alarm and panic," we learn, "by such developments as the great war record and tremendous postwar recovery of the Soviet

Union, the establishment of the People's Democracies in Eastern Europe, the historic victory of the Chinese People's Republic . . . and now, the frightening exposure of capitalist weakness in Korea and throughout Asia."

It was not noted that the Soviet achievements in eastern Europe and China were due to American co-operation or acquiescence. Nor was it pointed out that the uncertain outcome in Korea arose largely from the restraints which American foreign policy put upon the United States in the conduct of military operations. The idea was to resurrect "the spectre haunting Europe," to which Karl Marx had referred in the *Communist Manifesto* of 1848 and assure themselves and the world that it "has already become the victorious Soviet giant, gaining hourly in stature."

This Red propaganda about "Soviet might" got around, through concealed Communists and non-Communists. It was reflected in the memorandum of Owen Lattimore to the State Department as early as the fall of 1949. His recommendations included abandonment of Korea and Japan, and full recognition of Red China. Beyond that, and most significantly, Lattimore suggested that the United States avoid all "local entanglements" which might annoy Stalin. Since the Soviet dictator will be annoyed by the presence of the United States anywhere, including the United States itself, this was equivalent to eventual complete surrender. An argument for such suicidal conduct could only be that Soviet Russia is so powerful that our government dare not challenge the Kremlin in any area. This attitude was supported by the loud talk of "the danger of general war" and of atomic attack upon the United States should this country move in any firm way against Soviet expansion.

The acceptance of this view in official circles is summarized by the National Commander of the American Legion, Donald R. Wilson. His central theme, vigorously expressed, was that American strength on behalf of real peace had been "stultified because of the ivory tower concept of American diplomacy espoused during these days by our own incompetent State Department." This veteran of the Normandy landings of World War II declared that the United States had entered the Korean conflict in order to win real peace "by punishing the aggressor and by bringing about a unification of the political elements of the Korean peninsula." But this aim, which would have constituted a contribution to the peace of the world, was frustrated. Wilson said:

The American mind has not changed, but for some reason or another, the American government, or elements within that government, have presented to us a different set of objectives. They have told us that the original objectives we had in mind could not diplomatically be accomplished. They told us we could not fight on for victory, that our objective must be that of fighting an inconclusive engagement, of getting something less than victory in the killing of Chinese Communists and destroying Chinese communist forces in the field.

And the reasons given for this weakening of our hand in Korea, as recounted by the Legion's national commander, are precisely an echo of those legends of "Soviet invincibility" which the "Communists have been promoting in the American market of ideas during the whole "cold war" period. Speaking of those high in the government who advocated a stalemate war in Korea, Mr. Wilson said: "They told us that if we were to take those steps which would have meant victory in the field, that the Soviet Union would enter the conflict and that American cities very possibly and probably would be bombed and destroyed. They—these elements in government—told us that we had to temporize with the Russian threat," not bomb the Communist bases of equipment in Manchuria and not blockade the Chinese Communist coastline.

Thus a specter was raised in certain official circles in Washington, a creation of the imagination to frighten the American mind. It prevented us from carrying through those military objectives which are necessary to establish peace in the Far East and which we could have carried through. The threats of Soviet power to Korea and the American mainland were circulated in this country although the Soviet Union had admitted great difficulties in transporting supplies. Nowhere are these difficulties more pronounced than in the Far East, with a single track railroad of some 8,000 miles between the source and destination of supplies. At the same time, American strength and American potential production and power were completely discounted by those who endeavored to frighten us out of making an all-out effort in Korea.

The argument that Soviet Russia might provoke a general war and overrun the world if the United States took a firm stand against her aggression was heard also at the time of the Berlin Airlift. When in April 1948, the Russians shut off American food supplies and convoys of other materials from West Berlin, their purpose was clearly to force the Americans out of that sector. This was in clear violation of the Potsdam agreement, in which the United States had been naïvely lenient in granting Soviet Russia possession of the corridor leading to the American-occupied portion of the former German capital. As a result of the Soviet blockade, the American press immediately went into a state of "war scare." This had its effect. Instead of marching through the corridor, which existed solely because of its gift by the United States to Soviet Russia, American authorities decided upon conveying goods by air. While this was a great mechanical triumph for the United States, it indicated a political weakness, which could be interpreted only as a fear by our government of the might of Soviet Russia.

If this precedent is to be followed, then this country will be compelled to retreat in one form or another whenever the Soviet dictatorship chooses to challenge us or to conquer new lands. For it was based on a premise, bred of appeasement, that fails to take into account the vast potentialities of the United States and the internal weaknesses of the Soviet regime and its satellites.

It is true that Lavrenti P. Beria, important member of the Moscow Politburo, announced in late 1951 that Soviet steel production was then "about equal to the aggregate output of Britain, France, Belgium, and Sweden." This means that Soviet Russia will produce something like 35,000,000 tons of steel this year, if Beria's figures are correct. It is also true that in February 1946, when the Communists here were urging America to demobilize and cease war production, Stalin set new goals for immediate rebuilding of the Red Army and for industrial output. For steel, the Soviet dictator set a goal of 60,000,000 tons for 1960. But as Harry A. Schwartz has stated in his careful work, *Russia's Soviet Economy,* Soviet planning is subject to much "guesswork." Since Soviet figures are rigidly withheld from the outside world, they are also suspect. Granting, however, that Beria's estimates are correct, they still lag far behind the 105,000,000 tons of steel produced in the United States in 1951. And American production must be multiplied by our ability, if we have the will, to raise these figures much higher.

Of American potentialities in steel and other manufactured goods, the survey made by J. Frederick Dewhurst and Associates for the Twentieth Century Fund states:

The United States has reached such a high stage of industrial development that great quantities of facilities can be added in a short time—if there is a demand for their products. Indeed, in such industries as shipbuilding, it requires no longer to construct the facilities than to build the product. During the war, we increased our manufacturing facilities—though in a distorted fashion—by roughly fifty per cent. We were able to expand our productive capacity enormously and rapidly, devote almost half our economic effort to production for war, and still maintain a high living standard for the civilian population. We have more than enough manpower and resources and potential productive facilities to fulfill our requirements under every conceivable circumstance.

It can be readily recognized how vital it is to Stalin to interrupt this productive giant, the United States, by creating dissensions within our borders and by disrupting the economy through Red-instigated strikes. This has now become the announced purpose of the Soviet-controlled World Federation of Trade Unions, whose chief representative in this country is Harry Bridges, the organizer in 1951 of a conference to consider the formation of a Communist federation of labor unions. These hopes of Soviet Russia, not of coming near to American production but of halting it from within, throw new light upon the Communist Party's concentration policy in the basic industries, stressed by the Fifteenth National Convention of the Communist Party in December, 1950, and repeated in urgent directives throughout 1951. Therein, rather than in actual Soviet might, lies the real threat to our productive abilities and to our productive standing in the world.

The Achilles heel of the Soviet regime in the field of industrial production is the comparative inefficiency of its new ruling class and its dependence on slave labor. In addition, there is the labor passport system, the chaining of workers to their jobs, so that they may not move to new ones without the consent of the bureaucracy. While this has given Soviet Russia an apparent advantage in building up war production, since labor is ruthlessly forbidden to strike or otherwise take collective action, it is bound to prove a weakness in any great emergency. As Mr. Schwartz has stated, "the high hope once held that the Bolshevik Revolution might usher in an era of freedom and abundance has long since been destroyed. Deprived of political liberty, the Soviet masses have received neither economic liberty nor a satisfactory standard of living. Deceived by lies and cowed by the secret police, they are powerless as the fruits of their toil are diverted to support the new Soviet aristocracy and to maintain the largest military establishment in the world." [3] This is an unhealthy condition, which precludes the maximum loyalty and effort in any great crisis such as general war. It must not be forgotten, although it has largely been overlooked in the whole discussion of Soviet Russia, that three Soviet Republics and two autonomous territories were so overwhelmingly "treasonable" to the Kremlin in World War II that they had to be obliterated. Moscow officially announced the annihilation of these national units and the deportation of their populations to Siberia, even though the 1936 Stalin Constitution names them, and declares that each division of the Soviet Union is guaranteed the right of secession!

[3] *Russia's Soviet Economy* by Harry Schwartz, 1950.

The comparative inefficiency of the new Soviet ruling class and the widespread existence of slave labor have been presented in careful studies by David Dallin, in his books, *The Real Soviet Russia* and *Forced Labor in Soviet Russia*. It is surprising that these careful and scholarly works have received so little attention in official Washington. A reading of these books would have disclosed such realities as this: "Actually, the efficiency of forced labor, in spite of the incentives and compulsions, was and is on an extremely low level. The *average* efficiency of a slave laborer has certainly been below fifty per cent of that of a free Russian worker, whose productivity in turn has never been high."

If further evidence were wanted, it is supplied by the reports of the American Federation of Labor and the British government to the United Nations on the widespread and growing slave-labor camps in Soviet Russia and the satellites. Our leaders and the American people cannot ignore the fact that from fifteen to twenty million slaves exist in Soviet Russia alone, and that the system is developing rapidly in all satellite nations. This is such a flagrant violation of the Four Freedoms about which so much was said in World War II that the failure to raise this issue in a challenging way on the floor of the United Nations is virtually an act of appeasement.

As for the satellites, the surveys published in September, 1950, by the *Annals of the American Academy of Political and Social Science* are most revealing. Dr. Andrew Halasz, an authority on Southeastern European affairs, informs us that the Soviet system was so closely followed by the satellites "that the Communist governments in these countries established even its worst aspect —forced labor." And to this was promptly added the labor passport system for so-called "free" labor. As a result, Dr. Halasz declares:

The present situation of labor, resulting from the postwar policy of the Communist governments, is very bad. Its standard of living is low, less than half of the prewar standard. Its political status is even worse. The worker has lost his free vote in union elections, the protection of trade unions, the right to strike, the right to quit his job, and a fixed number of working hours, and finally he can be drafted for 'free' [without pay] and forced work at any time.

Real strength cannot exist under such conditions. They are, of course, in sharp contrast to the monotonously roseate pictures reported by the Cominform from the various satellite governments. It would be tedious to quote them all, but for illustration, in August, 1951, the report of G. Kliment, member of the central committee of the Communist Party in Czechoslovakia, describes "the labor enthusiasm of millions of workers" as "the guarantee that we will register more and more successes in building socialist industry." It tells of new and bigger factories being built and of a greater step-up of industrial output. It records "with gratitude" the direct scientific and technical aid accorded by Soviet Russia, and praises "Soviet technique and science" as far superior to that of the capitalists.

Shadows of reality are thrown across this picture of a new paradise, however, in admissions of the inadequate utilization of machinery, the need for "economy" which means additional reductions in living standards, and a significant reference to "the extremely swollen administrative apparatus of management boards." It is precisely this phenomenon—one group of management officials watching the other—that David Dallin points to as a weakness in the Soviet bureaucratic system. All of these bureaucrats, some of them receiving higher rewards in comparison to the masses than the captains of industry in the United States, have to be supported by the industries. That necessitates rigid rules against labor and enormous forced labor enterprises.

Only a few months after Kliment's enthusiastic version of Czechoslovakian development, the seriousness of the crisis there was announced to the world by the Communist regime itself. The arrest of Rudolf Slansky for "aiding the capitalists" constitutes an admission of failure that cannot be passed over lightly. Slansky was Moscow's representative in Czechoslovakia, and he had been given the honor of saluting Stalin on his seventieth birthday before the international Communist world. His arrest indicates serious differences of opinion among Communist leaders over difficulties of a vital nature.

Our officials, however, seem to be so impressed by Czech power that they are unable to secure the release of the American newspaperman, William N. Oatis, imprisoned there. And in the case of Robert Vogeler we dilly-dallied with Hungary for a year and a half before we obtained his release by inordinate concessions.

Confessions of economic weakness, arising from lack of "labor discipline," come also from Mattias Rakosi, general secretary of the Hungarian Communists. In his report, published in the December 7, 1951, issue of the Cominform's organ, Rakosi complains of the need of "strict observance of labor and State discipline."

"During recent months," he reports, "we placed the strengthening of labor discipline on the order of the day. Experience has shown that the measures taken so far have not yielded the desired result." He asserts that those who violate discipline "are treated gently, in liberal fashion" in too many cases. Such gentleness must be ended, he says, and the workers forced to work according to the orders of the State machine. The same applies to farmers, who are charged with refusing to pay taxes and sabotaging the quotas of grain which their Red masters demand from them. Not infrequently, Rakosi exclaims, "deliberate hostility" is shown by the people against the measures insisted upon by the Communist regime.

From the Supreme Headquarters of the Allied Powers in Europe at Rocquen, France, General of the Army Dwight D. Eisenhower adds his comment on Soviet "weakness": "We know something about their industrial limitations, their problems of transport and communications. We know many of the weaknesses they have as well as we know the terrifying strength they are building up in the form of military power." For that reason, Eisenhower thinks it doubtful that Soviet Russia would "provoke a global war," which in view of Stalin's progress with the creeping blitzkrieg (my term, not Eisenhower's) would seem to be the last thing Moscow would desire. The war that Stalin is now waging, conquering one small nation after another through concessions by the United States, is far better suited to his plans.

The myth of the productive and economic strength of Soviet Russia is matched by the fiction concerning the invincibility of the Red Army. As early as 1936, Marshal Tukhachevski (shot a few years later by Stalin's orders) boasted that "the frontiers of our socialist fatherland are impregnable." Three years later, Stalin was to assert that any foreign pigs putting their "snouts in our Soviet garden" would be dealt with ruthlessly. When Hitler on June 22, 1941, invaded the territories of his former ally, these predictions proved to be mere bombast. This has been well shown by Father Leopold Braun, A.A., who was practically the only American to remain in Moscow throughout Hitler's advance. He gives an account of "fleeing Red officers and soldiers," instantly accused of treason as the only excuse that could be offered for the shattered prestige of the Red Army. He says that within ten days after Hitler's armies crossed the Russian borders through the Baltic states, "Red Army resistance was so ineffective that *Narkoms* [departmental chiefs] had hastily flown out" of the big cities that stood in the path of the advancing Nazi armies. The retreat, he reports, was like that of a mob, "certainly anything but a planned affair. Red Army men in several instances had to be pushed into battle by the bayonets of the NKVD troops." When there was no danger of being shot by the Soviet secret police troops, they went over in droves to the Germans. Father Braun asserts that only these "torturers of the people" prevented "a global insurrection" behind the lines in Soviet Russia.[4]

It was the NKVD troops, furnished and fed by United States aid, who arrested and shot down the young Russian soldiers returning home from the lands they had invaded and reporting on the superior development of these Western countries. These men were branded traitors for their reports, many of them shot, the rest sent off to hard labor in prison camps.

"In the light of these details," Father Braun writes in the *American Legion Magazine,* for October, 1951, "the might of the Red Army becomes a myth, its strength a weakness—because all is based on systematized fear and bullying. Stalin and the Politburo know this better than anyone else. Never will they risk sending the Red Army into world conflict because of its inherent instability."

[4] "The Myth of the Mighty Red Army," by the Reverend Leopold Braun, *American Legion Magazine,* October, 1951.

Their attack upon the United States will never come until by periphery warfare and infiltration they have so weakened this nation and spread defeatism within its borders that it can collapse.

Putting all legends and propaganda aside, it was the United States that saved the Soviet regime in World War II. The Kremlin was well aware of this and constantly urged the American Communists to hasten the coming of help. Now by direction of the Kremlin they are telling a different story. We must not become the victims of their carefully planned effort to convince us that the Soviet Union, with its many glaring weaknesses, is a power too great for us to challenge. The United States is infinitely stronger. To surrender at every step of the way to Soviet demands because of the fictitious "threat of war" is to throw away the powerful advantage we have, demoralize ourselves, and lose the opportunity to lead the world toward freedom.

# CHAPTER 10

# *The Road to Peace*

At the Palais de Chaillot in Paris, almost right up to Christmas, 1951, a debate raged in the United Nations Assembly which concluded in "a major propaganda defeat for the Kremlin." That is what most of our press termed the vote on the disarmament plan submitted by the Western Powers.

It was frankly acknowledged that Secretary of State Dean Acheson had put the plan before the General Assembly because of pressure on the State Department to offset the mounting Soviet "peace" campaign. This world-wide appeal to the nations outside the Iron Curtain, as we have noted, proposed complete surrender to the Kremlin as the price of "peace," since it entailed terms which would wholly disarm the United States and other non-Soviet nations. But its effect among the European peoples was sufficient to slow down their defense preparations, which could be one of the guarantees for halting the extension of World War III. Anne O'Hare McCormick, a month before the vote on the disarmament proposal, had admitted in the New York *Times* that "everyone concerned with the defense of the West seems to have come to the same conclusion . . . that the program needs to be revised." Mrs. McCormick alluded to Secretary Acheson's disarmament proposal as one of the major items in this revision, and also to the trip of General Eisenhower to Washington to review the situation and the special Ottawa conference on the North Atlantic Treaty Organization. "These developments combine with others," Mrs. McCormick wrote, "to indicate that we are at another turning point on the weary but widening road toward world order."

The Soviet cries of "warmongering" and "imperialist" adventures" demanded an answer. A proposal of worldwide disarmament was the answer by the United States, Great Britain, and France, to be accomplished gradually through a disarmament commission, and with provisions for inspection of the arms pile and military build-up in every country. The latter suggestion aroused the ire of the Soviet delegation, as was to be expected, since the Kremlin maintains the Iron Curtain for the purpose of hiding what it is doing militarily as well as shutting off its slave camps and exploited populations from the view of the rest of the world. In reply, the Soviet representatives demanded the immediate and complete prohibition of atomic weapons, and a one-third reduction of the armed forces of the five big powers—all this to be done prior to any consideration of inspection. This, of course, would result in a fully armed Soviet Russia with the rest of the world disarmed. An overwhelming vote in the Assembly against this preposterous proposal and for the Western recommendation, was "the major success" to which so many of our newspapers referred.

Sober second thought considerably discounted this view. Andrei Vishinsky took much of the propaganda value out of the vote by immediately charging the United States with initiating and encouraging subversion in the satellite nations. In view of the Kremlin's long record of fifth columns, espionage, and general interference in other nations, the insolence of this charge could hardly be surpassed. Almost simultaneously with it, the McCarran Subcommittee was criticizing the State Department for permitting the free passage of American Communists to Moscow, charging that this strengthened the courier and espionage system of Soviet Russia. But the American representatives at the Paris meeting, including Mr. Acheson and Dr. Philip C. Jessup, did not hurl into the teeth of the Soviet delegation the long bill of particulars they could have assembled on Soviet subversion in every country of the world. They chose to let the United States go on trial, only asserting that the charges were false and could be successfully disproved.

This agreement to let the United States be tried before the world for alleged subversion in exploited and subjugated nations gave Soviet Russia the opportunity for a new attack, this time on the subject of infiltration and internal conspiracy. Even James Reston of the New York *Times,* long regarded as an apologist for the State Department, at this point became critical. The State Department would have been on more solid ground, Mr. Reston observed, had it declared the charges impertinent, "coming from the center of the greatest fifth columns in history." If there was to be a debate on the matter, he thought, the United States should have insisted that "the subversive activities of the Soviet Union be included in the debate." [1]

Mr. Reston gave a strange twist to his remarks by comparing Secretary Acheson's claim that Vishinsky's charges are "spurious and false" with Dr. Jessup's denial that the State Department ever considered the recognition of Red China. The Acheson disclaimer of aid to the

[1] New York *Times,* December 20, 1951.

democratic elements in eastern Europe is the repudiation of a merit—of what should and must be the American action if there is ever to be peace in the world. To permit Stalin to consolidate his power over the satellite regimes in eastern Europe and China is not only to agree to the destruction of the Four Freedoms among these peoples; it is also an assurance that the Kremlin will be able to expand the sweep of warfare across Europe and Asia and eventually attack the Western Hemisphere. The United States has an obligation to prevent such a development by raising the question of these nations on the floor of the United Nations and encouraging the restlessness which exists.

The Jessup assertion was an effort to conceal an egregious error, or worse, from the American people. The Reston criticism, coming from a friend of the State Department, is an important admission of our official acceptance of moves which aid Soviet psychological and military warfare. This acceptance is particularly distressing when you consider the character of some of the Soviet "peace" propaganda. In the October 10, 1951, issue of *New Times* of Moscow, which gives directives to all Communist leaders, Joseph Stalin's statement of the previous February was republished for world-wide circulation. Here the dictator remarks that the experiences of Britain and the United States prove that "increasing the armed forces of a country, and the drive for armaments, lead to expansion of the war industry, curtailment of civilian industry, suspension of big civilian construction works, higher taxes, and higher prices for articles of mass consumption." The Moscow paper goes on to hold the specter of this dire fate over the peoples of Europe, if they consent to defense preparations. The United

States, of course, appears as the villain, persuading Europe to this catastrophic course.

Neither Stalin, nor the *New Times,* nor the Communist echoes of them throughout the world, refers to the real fact, that Soviet aggression is making American preparedness necessary. On the contrary, the *New Times* quotes Stalin in a new interview to the effect that "the Soviet Union has no intention of ever attacking the USA or any other country."

These words, contradicting the set objectives of the Kremlin to establish a world Soviet dictatorship, are ordered to be peddled by Communists among the peoples of the world, including those of Europe. And while such fictions are being distributed far and wide, picturing "American imperialism" as the cause of a future war, the United States will be put on trial before the world for the crime of encouraging "subversion." She will be on the defensive even in the United Nations.

The road to real peace, it is clear, does not lie only through preparedness and gifts for the rehabilitation of other nations. The Marshall Plan did much to revive Europe, but its effect will be largely dissipated if it is not accompanied by the real key to world peace: Initiative in the hands of the United States at all times against the predatory acts of Soviet Russia and deeds by the United States that will give confidence to other nations.

In the fall of 1938, a gentleman with an umbrella descended from a plane in England to announce that he had assured "peace in our time." What he had made absolutely sure was war. The blunder of Neville Chamberlain can be repeated. Our danger, in the light of events of 1945 to 1951, is that it will be. The historian, Theodor Mommsen, commenting on events in ancient Rome, sagely remarks: "If a garrison will not fight, walls and moats are of no avail." The American people have demonstrated that they will fight for their liberties and their country, but they require (as do all peoples) a leadership that will definitely and firmly point the way.

The outstanding recommendation of measures to insure peace came from the American Legion's national convention at Miami in October, 1951. After vigorously applauding the statement of General Douglas Mac-Arthur, its guest of honor, that "the best presently available assurance of world peace is to have in the hands of this great peace-loving nation the mightiest armament in the world," the convention passed a resolution condemning "the failure of the State Department to deal adequately with the grim and bloody advance of Communism." The delegates understood, that is, that essential as full preparedness was, without a firm policy it would not be effective. The Legion further demanded the removal from the State Department, and from all government departments, "of any and all persons who are not in complete accord with our opposition to Communism," and their replacement by men of "unquestioned loyalty, with realistic views and unquestioned courage." [2]

This sharply worded recommendation, made even sharper by the debate and adopted almost unanimously, points up the need for a thorough overhauling of our State Department as the number one step on the path to genuine peace. When Stalin learns that the United States will not acquiesce in every demand he makes, but will seize and retain the initiative, then the Soviet Union will retreat. Long ago, the master of the Kremlin wrote that "Communists must be experts in the art of retreat," and

[2] Summary of Proceedings, Thirty-Third Annual Convention of the American Legion, Miami, Florida, October 15 to 18, 1951, page 86.

the opportunity should be given them to practice this art.

Since the adoption of the American Legion resolution, the Lisbon meeting has taken place, which agreed upon the formation of armies for the North Atlantic Treaty Organization. This was acclaimed as an achievement by Secretary of State Acheson, and not without justification, for international negotiations are not easy in the present scene. Unfortunately, however, the Lisbon meeting was followed very shortly by a crisis in France which caused that country to hesitate at fulfilling its commitments to the NATO. And we cannot close our eyes to the fact that this misfortune was in part a product of American appeasement. The French crisis, which the Communists hope to use as a means of penetrating the NATO Army if it is ever organized, is at bottom a victory for the "peace partisans" directed from Moscow. The Cominform organ for December 14, 1951, boasts of "numerous delegations of French peace supporters visiting the United Nations" when it was in session at the Palais de Chaillot. Throughout France at the same time local "peace congresses" were held, with attacks upon the United States and demands for recognition of Red China and "support of the Soviet Union's peace proposals." In every municipality Communist-led "peace groups" are continually pressing for "trade between France and the Soviet Union and the people's democracies"—an effort to channel the benefits of the Marshall Plan into helping the shaking economies of the Soviet satellites.

What is important for us is that these French organizations are encouraged by the so-called "peace partisans" in the United States. Constant reports are received in France as to what is happening in "the American peace movement." All these things are closely connected.

The State Department has been anything but alert in preventing the poison of local Red propaganda against the United States from reaching France. It permitted William L. Patterson of the Civil Rights Congress, a notorious Red, to travel to the United Nations meeting at Paris in 1951. He presented there a report charging "genocide" to the American nation. This charge, based upon excesses growing out of the Negro problem here, has now been published in pamphlet form for distribution throughout the world. It could not but create a bad effect among the French, harassed by the interminable conflict in Indo-China, and easy to persuade that American attitudes toward the colored races make their difficulties greater.

The Negro problem in America is indeed a challenge to our democracy. We certainly cannot blame Soviet propaganda for the fact that such a problem exists and that we must do something effective about it. But that does not justify the criminally false use the Communists make of it. Their dishonesty in this matter has been well exposed recently by the Reverend William A. Nolan in his book, *Communism versus the Negro.*

It was not until Patterson had returned from Paris— that is, after the damage was done—that the State Department "lifted" his passport. A number of other Communists have been permitted to go freely to European countries and to Soviet Russia during the past few years, spreading hatred for the United States wherever they go. In another way United States officials have played the game of the appeasement forces within France. That is, by casting aspersions on the Franco regime in Spain while sending millions of dollars to bolster the Communist regime of Tito in Yugoslavia. Such attitudes strengthen those who wish to compromise with Communism and "do business with Stalin." Moreover, Red hopes of infiltration in the NATO armies, and other organizations vital to its development, are not checked by the indifference of leading circles in the State Department to security risks within its own personnel.

In connection with the long-delayed ouster of John Stewart Service from our diplomatic service, the columnist Fulton Lewis, Jr., remarks that the President's Loyalty Review Board has more work on its hands. He refers specifically to Dr. Philip C. Jessup, who participated in the agreement to let the United States be put on trial before the United Nations. "So far, Senator Pat McCarran's investigation of the Institute of Pacific Relations," writes Mr. Lewis, "has turned up forty-four Reds in the organization, and that is only about half of them. Jessup dealt with all of them, although he has denied he knew they were Communists, with the exception of his friend, Frederick V. Field. And it was years before he would believe even that." A man with such color blindness can scarcely be considered a good security risk or competent to detect the maneuvers of the Kremlin.

Others under investigation, according to Mr. Lewis, were O. Edmund Clubb, until recently head of the State Department's China desk, and Dr. Esther Caukin Brunauer, also employed as a State Department official. Dr. Brunauer was under charges of friendly relations with Communists and of friendly acts to pro-Communist causes, when she was cleared in 1950 by the Tydings Committee. Now she has been suspended because of the discovery of "new evidence." In the case of Clubb, Dean Acheson has admitted that he cleared him after the State Department's own loyalty board had found him a doubtful security risk.

Here is how the process is described by Mr. Lewis:

"So it goes. First, the accusation, then the bleat of total innocence from all hands, especially the State Department, and then later the suspension." And it might be inserted, as part of this process, that a campaign of character assassination is frequently unloosed against those naming the person whose loyalty is questioned.

The American Legion resolution indicates that the suspension, or even the discharge of such persons, while helpful, is not enough. The cleaning up that will dedicate the State Department to a genuine defense of American security must start from the top and work down. A thorough-going revision of mood and attitude is required, a change from negative to positive, from passive to active. Nothing but a complete overhauling of the department's personnel and leadership can produce this change. That is the meaning of the Legion resolution.

It is supported by the fact that those who influenced the State Department from 1944 to 1951 continue to influence it. Owen Lattimore, who had so much to do with the tragic Chinese policy, was on a special mission to Afghanistan for the United Nations in 1950 when he was recalled to appear before the Tydings Committee. He could hardly have been commissioned to study such a critical area, in the path of Stalin's potential moves southward, without the approval of the State Department. The attitude with which he approached his task may be learned from an article in the *Communist* for November, 1944, outlining with approval an article of his in the *Far Eastern Survey,* an organ of the Institute of Pacific Relations. There Lattimore sought to answer the question: "What would happen if one of these Soviet minorities were to attempt to set up laws, institutions, and practices conflicting with Marxist doctrines and Soviet orthodoxy?" History had already given the answer in the ruthless purges of the Soviet dictatorship. But Lattimore had a different answer: "This would be the last thing that would occur to their minds, not the first. . . . Since, in all their long history, only the Soviet government ever freed them from discrimination and gave them the opportunity of progress, they identify their own interests with the Soviet interests." The "instinct" of these minority nationalities is therefore "to advance the general Soviet interest" since it is bound up with their own. That is the kind of man chosen by the State Department to advise us about affairs in Asia. Peace cannot be won until our State Department is in other hands. That is the first change that must be made.

Second, we must stop paying blackmail to the Kremlin or its satellite regimes. We should, indeed, demand the expulsion of these satellites from the United Nations, if they persist in their brigandage against American citizens. Robert A. Vogeler, the American businessman imprisoned for over a year in Red Hungary, would endorse such a policy. "Although I was happy to gain my own freedom, I was shocked to learn that the United States had to pay ransom," he said. To win Vogeler's release, after he had been framed by the Hungarian Communists, the State Department agreed that Hungarian consulates should be reopened here, that American citizens should be permitted to travel in Hungary, and that Hungarian property taken by the Nazis should be given the Communist government. These satellite consulates are espionage nests, and the permission for Americans to travel in Hungary meant only that Communists should be allowed to go there and get directives for their work against the United States. Other Americans would obviously be in danger of new kidnappings and new demands for ransom.

Mr. Vogeler charged that the Reds in Hungary were preparing another indignity against Americans in November when they declared that the United States had failed to live up to the terms of ransom for his freedom. That new indignity soon materialized in the shooting down and arrest of four American fliers and the imposing upon them of fines amounting to $120,000. This holdup was even cruder than the acts of the Barbary pirates which even the youthful American Republic would not let go unpunished. "We have let ourselves be intimidated," Vogeler said. "The only way to gain release for hostages is to take the strong way and don't give in."

The American Legion outlined this "strong way" in the case of the American newspaperman, William N. Oatis, kidnapped and imprisoned by the Czechoslovak Reds, demanding that the United States shut down all the Czechoslovak Red consulates in this country, cut off all trade with Czechoslovakia, and demand the expulsion of that satellite from the United Nations.

If these moves were made, others would surely follow on a large scale. We should insist that our allies stand up with us, Great Britain specifically withdrawing its recognition of Red China. We should start an all-out campaign, backing it up with action, for the unification of Korea on a democratic basis and the unification of Germany on the same terms. With that would go genuine co-operation with Chiang Kai-shek, and an end to all restrictions on his operations against the Chinese Communists.

We should push vigorously the recommendation made by Representative Charles Kersten of Wisconsin that the exiles from the satellite states be organized to conduct opposition to the Red regimes within their homelands. To further this, we should protest vigorously on the

floor of the United Nations the outrages committed by
these Kremlin puppets. Their expulsion would be the
result, if the Four Freedoms still have any meaning.
That might lead to a break with Soviet Russia, which,
as the columnist David Lawrence has said, is inevitable
in view of Soviet acts, and would be logical. If it is
argued that such a program would lead to war—and that
has been the major argument in favor of appeasement—
the answer is that our policies have got us into such a
poor position that there is no road to peace except at
the risk of war. But the economic weakness of Soviet
Russia and the difficulty of keeping the oppressed populations from revolt make such an outcome improbable.

In tune with these external measures we should out-
law the Communist Party at home. This also was demanded by the American Legion and by many other
organizations. It has not been achieved because of the
foolish argument, originated by the Communists, that
this security measure would lead to "police-state rule."
In the September, 1950 issue of *Political Affairs,* Alexander Bittelman, chief theoretician of the Communist
Party and a Soviet subject, instructs the comrades to
spread the idea that any restriction of the Communists
would lead to "fascism." In the same breath, he writes
that the Communist Party "is inspired and guided by
the teachings of Marxism-Leninism," which demand the
forcible overthrow and "smashing" of the United States
government, as both V. I. Lenin and Joseph Stalin have
emphatically stated.

Despite the origin of this idea in the camp of those
very Reds who plan to destroy all democratic rights and
liberties, it has spread far and wide. By December 18,
1951, Elizabeth Gurley Flynn could exultantly report
in the *Daily Worker* that Americans for Democratic

Action had declared for the repeal of the Smith Act, under which the eleven Communist leaders were convicted. She could also refer to the resolution adopted by the National Convention of the CIO, although she exaggerated its terms. This resolution criticized the Smith Act. Only a year before the CIO had expelled Communist-controlled unions and presented an indictment against them for their subversive activities—a move strangely inconsistent with the resolution criticizing the Smith Act. As the Smith Act is the sole present means of dealing with the fifth column, the zeal of the Communists to have it repealed is understandable. It is the more regrettable that non-Communist groups have joined this demand. We must remember, however, that the CIO originally defended the Red leader, Harry Bridges, and the Soviet agent, John Santo, and had in its national headquarters such pro-Communists as Lee Pressman, Len DeCaux, and others. It changed its attitude sharply on all these persons, condemning Bridges and discharging Pressman and DeCaux. Its censure of the Smith Act may too be subject to change, when CIO leaders see the wide and harmful use the Reds will make of it. In the opinion of Victor Riesel, syndicated columnist on labor, that vote of censure did not represent the view of the CIO as a whole, but of a determined minority.

One of the most encouraging events of recent years was precisely the condemnation and expulsion of Communist-controlled unions from the CIO in 1949 and 1950. The reports of the committees which tried these Red-ruled unions indicate how vital it is that the legitimate labor movement be upheld in its contest with the Communists. In the report recommending the expulsion of the American Communications Association, headed by Joseph P. Selly, we read:

Throughout this curious history [of constant support to the Communist line], the Communist Party has never ceased to claim that it makes its decisions on the basis of a genuine appraisal of the interests of the American people and of American labor. That claim is, of course, false. The record shows that the basic purpose of the Communist Party is the support of the Soviet Union and that the program of the party is designed with only the interests of the Soviet Union in view. . . . The Communist Party's single-minded devotion to Russia controls its position on domestic issues as well as on matters of foreign policy. A peculiar and consistent characteristic of the Communist Party program is that it always finds a tie-in between domestic and foreign policy.

In regard to the Red attitude toward unions, the committee stated:

It [the committee] finds that, although the Communist Party has claimed to champion unionism and organization, it has always done so in order to carry on Communist work within trade unions and in order to pervert their policies to the advantage of the Soviet Union. The Communist Party, the committee finds, does not believe in trade unions. It believes in using trade unions. And it believes in using them for the purposes of the Soviet Union.

Every one of the CIO committees trying Red-controlled unions stated these same facts in their findings. In each case, too, the union involved was found guilty of the same practices described as follows in the charge against the American Communications Association: "From this examination, the committee finds that the policies and activities of the ACA have followed and continue to follow exactly, without deviation, the program of the Communist Party." Such findings, each concluding with a denunciation of the union as a Communist creature, disloyal to CIO policies and objectives, give hope that the censure of the Smith Act by the CIO will be only temporary. The ability of Communist cells to expand whenever opportunity presents, and their skillful use of non-Communist citations to defend such expansion, make this reversal important not only to the country, but to the CIO.

Objection is often raised to outlawing the Communist Party on the ground that this would drive the Communists underground. The fact is that the party has always been ninety-five per cent underground. It has also had the advantage, however, of legality, of the open functioning of that part of its apparatus which runs newspapers, uses telephones, and has offices. Through this small "open" part, a stream of instructions and contacts proceeds from the Soviet agents, who rule the "party" underground, to the great numbers of concealed Communists operating publicly as non-Communists.

Since these "non-Communists" strive above all to penetrate government positions, it follows that effective security regulations for government employees are essential to a vigorous anti-Communist program. Former Senator Hiram Bingham, chairman of the Loyalty Review Board, has recommended that "security" rather than "disloyalty" be the criterion in passing upon these employees. In his opinion, all security as well as loyalty cases should come under the jurisdiction of the board which he heads. At present, only cases involving "loyalty" come under it. The Bingham recommendation is sound. As long as "loyalty" is the criterion, there is no effective protection of the government against infiltration. To sustain a charge of disloyalty, particularly under the methods of concealment used by the Communists, required endless time and often impossible effort. The pur-

pose is to defend the security of the nation, rather than
to penalize individuals. There are countless cases in
which bad associations, apparent stupidity, or indiscre-
tion, and what seem to be loose methods of work, are as
fatal as any proof of "disloyalty" could make them. This
has been made obvious by the recent presidential executive order which changed the basis of discharge from the
necessity of finding "reasonable grounds" for disloyalty
to the finding of "reasonable doubt" as to loyalty. To
extend this further, as Chairman Bingham suggests, and
make "security" the basis for Loyalty Review Board
action, is most essential. Under the old regulations, 1800
employees quit voluntarily rather than be subject to
questioning, which is proof enough of the need for more
extensive and intensive investigations.

The so-called "concentration policy" adopted by the
Reds and now being expanded, will have to be met with
more drastic measures, and defeated. This concentration policy calls for penetration of trade unions and all
organizations in communities connected with the basic
industries. Paralysis of American production, when such
will be helpful to Stalin, is the design. Great assistance
was given to this Red plan in 1951 by the decision of the
National Labor Relations Board to take at their face
value the oaths of Communist leaders in the Red-ruled
unions that they were non-Communist. Within a short
time thereafter, such veteran Reds as Ben Gold of the
International Fur and Leather Goods Union, Donald
Henderson of the Distributive Workers Union, Max Perlow of the Furniture Workers Union, and others, publicly resigned from the Communist Party. The *Daily
Worker* gave conspicuous space to these resignations,
which it would have denounced had they been genuine,
and assured the comrades that those who resigned would

continue "fraternal relations" with the party. It even boldly stated that the leaders were obliged to take this action in order to preserve their position in the mass organizations. In other words, they had technically resigned in order to take the non-Communist oath required by the Taft-Hartley Act.

While there are some good grounds for criticism of that act, the provision for the non-Communist oath, if properly enforced, would hit the conspiracy a hard blow. *Counterattack,* the alert weekly newsletter devoted to the activities of the party and its friends, urged the National Labor Relations Board to look behind these sudden resignations by these veteran Communists and pass upon their "good faith." But the NLRB chose another course. As a result, the Communists gained in the labor field in 1951, and are in a good position to shut down wide areas of production much better than in 1950, when after the expulsions from the CIO they were at their lowest ebb in labor organizations. The several unions, including the National CIO, which the Communists have persuaded to condemn the Smith Act, have opened the door for a new Red infiltration. If the members of Stalin's conspiracy are to be considered a part of the labor movement (which they plan to destroy), opposition to them is, of course, greatly weakened. And a condemnation of the Smith Act is tantamount to a declaration of their right to belong to it.

Efforts are now being made to plug one loophole in the Taft-Hartley Law through the introduction of House Bill HR 4680 requiring union officers to swear under oath every year that they are not CP members, are not affiliated with the CP, and have not been for the preceding twelve months. This is aimed at Harry Bridges and his Red colleagues, who met in October, 1951, to work

out plans for extending their power in the labor movement. A tape recording of their meeting shows that
Bridges proposed arbitrary strikes in sugar and other
fields, which would affect market prices. By tipping off
gamblers on the impending strikes, the party could make
thousands of dollars. Methods of arousing opposition to
the defense program were also discussed at this secret
meeting, which indicates that the Reds have great confidence that their infiltration apparatus is in good order.

It is quite obvious that this infiltration must be halted
if American opinion is to be mobilized for defense, and
if our foreign policy is to be keyed to the realities of
defense. In recent months Moscow has intensified its directives to Communists throughout the world in two
directions. First to steel their wills, increase their vigilance, heighten their "Bolshevik discipline." In this they
are to model themselves on the mother party, the Communist Party of the Soviet Union, and look to Stalin
for their leadership and guidance. The second directive
is to "strengthen their ties with the masses"—which is the
stock Communist phrase for wider infiltration. Unless
the outlawing of the Communist Party is accompanied
by alert and informed moves in every community against
Communist fronts and against Communist penetration
of other organizations, American public opinion will be
kept confused and bewildered, a condition helpful to
appeasement and leading to ultimate defeat.

Reminding us of this fact, Dr. J. B. Matthews made
public in December, 1951, a shocking list of current films
participated in by recently exposed Communists and collaborators with Communist fronts. This infiltration continues to flourish, notwithstanding the long investigations conducted by the House Committee on Un-American Activities from the time Dr. Matthews was associated

with that body to the present day. "Hundreds of motion picture celebrities," says Dr. Matthews, "have taken emphatic and public stands which were either out-and-out pro-Communist or which had the effect of aiding and abetting the Communist conspiracy. With very few exceptions, these same celebrities have not taken a similarly emphatic and public stand against the Communist menace, even to this very day in 1951." And that observation can be applied to all other opinion-making agencies in which small but aggressive and influential minorities of Communists and pro-Communists are working with disastrous results.

This is borne out, again, by Herbert Philbrick, who entered the Massachusetts Communist Party under the direction of the FBI. In January, 1952, Mr. Philbrick declared correctly that despite some defections, the Communist conspiracy is stronger now than it was a few years back and that the main source of its strength is the "pro" groups, that is, groups of professional people penetrating innocent organizations or aiding in the formation of Communist fronts. In spite of all the hullabaloo over "the Communist menace," these people continue to function at full force and, when exposed, to rally distinguished citizens to their defense.

If the United States is to survive, it will have to take a strong and astutely intelligent stand both against Stalin abroad and against his agents at home. In connection with the humiliating farce enacted around our fliers in Hungary, the commentator, David Lawrence, remarked:

As long as the Communists think that the American government will not take drastic action, they will continue to challenge American policy at every turn, and will seek methods to bring humiliation on the United States government before the European world. . . . Sooner or later the American government will have to stand up to that challenge, or face a constant deterioration of American prestige throughout the world.

For "American prestige," we might well substitute "American security" or "the possibility of assuring American defense," for if we do not stand up to the challenge, we lose the battle for the minds of the people in France, Italy, Germany, everywhere.

The Marshall Plan gave us a temporary advantage in Western Europe, but in the long run it is not possible to buy allies. They have to be won by confidence in our strength and purposes. In December 1947, when the Marshall Plan was before the Senate Appropriations Committee, General Albert E. Wedemeyer, representing the Chiefs of Staff, urged that funds for European recovery be preceded or accompanied by adequate arrangements for military preparedness. His suggestion was not adopted, but we know now how wise it was. As part of a firm and consistent policy, it would have spared us the present uncertainties of the North Atlantic Treaty Organization.

On February 23, 1952, John Foster Dulles, in an address at Princeton University, declared the plight of the West to be grave indeed. "As things now stand," he said, "the prospects are not encouraging from the standpoint of the free world." That same week he had said on a television program: "The tide is running against us. We seem to be on the defensive and they [the Russians] on the offensive. You can look around the whole circle of the world and find one spot after another where the question is: are we going to lose this part of the free world?"

Spruille Braden, former Assistant Secretary of State and Ambassador to Cuba and Argentina, also on February

23, 1952, denounced American policy for not standing up strongly against Soviet Russia. Braden went so far as to state that General MacArthur was withdrawn because he wanted to win the war.

These are the statements of men who have been intimately connected with the policy-making of our government.

Stalin's reluctance to march on Western Europe was due as much to weaknesses in his own camp as to the Marshall Plan. The difficulties confronting the Communist Party of France were stressed by Maurice Thorez, then its general secretary, as early as June 1945, two years before the Marshall Plan was suggested. The penetration of "alien ideas" into its ranks was scathingly criticized by the French Communist leader. "We still have need to exercise vigilance!" Thorez exclaimed at the Tenth Congress of the French party. "We must combat the opportunist, liquidationist concepts of certain people who think, without always clearly formulating it, that 'we have passed beyond the stage of the class struggle.'" Still more significantly, Thorez warned against the spreading from "the masses of workers and peasants" into the Communist ranks of ideas hostile to the objectives of the Soviet dictatorship.[3] Similar problems were raised by Palmiro Togliatti, leader of the Italian Communists. Clearly the Kremlin was aware that the conquest of Western Europe would present countless internal problems, especially if we gave "the masses of workers and peasants" confidence in our anti-Communist stand. Unfortunately we did not take advantage of this opportunity.

The world-wide "peace campaign," which Stalin de-

[3] "Organizational Problems of the Communist Party in France," by Maurice Thorez, *Political Affairs*, August, 1945; report to the Tenth National Convention of the Communist Party of France, on June 26, 1945.

vised in 1947 to overcome these weaknesses, has gone to extreme lengths to impress the masses. He went so far as to pass a law against "warmongering" within Soviet Russia, and have the Communists publicize it throughout the world. The United States should have exposed and denounced the hollow mockery of this alleged law. The floor of the United Nations is used continuously by the Soviet delegation to promote attacks on other nations. The United States should use it to expose the bankruptcy of all Soviet claims—from the pretense that a murderous dictatorship is "the highest stage of democracy" to the fictitious provision against anti-Semitism.

If peace is to be won, a rebirth of the duties of citizenship is required in the United States. And this means more than merely casting a ballot on election day. It means more than adopting such reforms as are essential to keep our democracy on a sound basis—a subject with which this book cannot deal. It means that all intelligent persons in every community must advise themselves critically and well on the nature and methods of the communist conspiracy to destroy our civilization. Just as the average American has been able to solve engineering, production, and economic problems whenever emergencies demanded it, so he must solve the political problem of World War III. He cannot endlessly permit it to go to Stalin by default. Unless alert citizens in every community study this matter seriously, combat the concealed Communists and their friends—no matter how powerfully placed—and bring pressure on the government to stop vacillating and end appeasement, that is how it will go.

We have failed to defeat the Kremlin's plans for "a series of bloody conflicts" with us (predicted by Stalin twenty-four years ago) because we have not understood the nature of Soviet Communism. It is the outgrowth of a philosophy of materialism, which denies the existence of God and the world of the spirit. Each of the Communist "scientists," as they are called—Marx, Engels, Lenin, and Stalin—has proclaimed dialectic materialism in nature and historical materialism in society as the Red world outlook. In the mass of matter in which the animal (man) functions, there is, according to this philosophy, a dialectical development at work. Its agency of progress is organized and systematized violence. From this belief flows logically the ruthless savagery of the Soviet dictatorship, its wholesale executions and enslavements.

But this materialist philosophy of violence does not stop there. It declares that the process must inevitably continue until a world-wide dictatorship of the same kind is achieved. Until then there can be no rest or peace for mankind. After its triumph, however, there will be ushered in a "classless society," or earthly paradise, where men will no longer be in conflict.

The fanaticism which this philosophy gives to the Communists, the fierce determination to destroy everything that stands in the path of the world dictatorship, has not been understood by Americans. They have not realized that the Soviet dictatorship will permit no peace in the world, since its whole conception of peace requires the violent destruction of everything non-Soviet.

A clear-eyed understanding of the road down which dialectic materialism leads will sharpen American estimates of Soviet maneuvers. It will make us realize that with such a foe, nothing can be gained by appeasement. Peace can result only from a strong moral initiative by the United States on all fronts.

# Index